PRAISE FOR
THE JOURNEYMAN LIFE

"This superb work transcends the 'ordinary' self-help book by inviting you on a unique voyage of self-discovery and deep introspection. Tony Daloisio not only asks the hard questions, he also models and shows us how to honestly face the difficult, even ugly parts of life (past or present) that we often try to avoid. Yet, it is only through this critical workout of our inner and outer selves that a true transformation takes place. And soon we'll discover—or rediscover—the real meaning of inside out. An enlightening and remarkable book written by an equally remarkable human being."

—**STEPHEN M. R. COVEY**, *New York Times* and #1 *Wall Street Journal* bestselling author of *The Speed of Trust* and *Trust and Inspire: How Truly Great Leaders Unleash Greatness in Others*

"Very few men have the courage to speak of, speak into, and speak about their journey of discovery and change because it requires transparency and vulnerability regarding the inner man. Into this vacuum of masculine dialogue comes a courageous river of authenticity and insight from one of us that you can trust. Please do not read *The Journeyman Life* for information. Read it for transformation. Be brave."

—**KENNY LUCK**, Founder and President of Every Man Ministries

"*The Journeyman Life* is potent wisdom for our times. With courage and compassion, Tony enters life's crises as sacred portals to inner growth and change. His journey treads the vulnerable path of transformation, revealing the importance of befriending our imperfections and the key to changing the world that is waiting to be found inside."

—**BARBARA VACARR**, CEO of Kripalu

"With breathtaking honesty, Tony puts himself on the examination table for, as he calls it, a full body scan. Then he invites us to do the same. His call to action is both frightening and exhilarating . . . If life is about change, which I believe it is, *The Journeyman Life* is a worthy resource to guide us on that journey. We can either change or tell ourselves stories about why we don't need to change. But even when we have the courage to see the unedited reality of our lives, we need help. This book is a marvelous source for that help."

—**TIM CLARK**, Founder and CEO of LeaderFactor

"Tony combines ancient wisdom with modern psychology and his own personal journey to map out a clear and in-depth path to doing the work as a man. Right now is the time to pick up this book and start your journey of inner work—you need it, and the world needs it as well! Our systems have been built on patriarchal mindsets, and the only way to heal our world, is to heal our masculinity. Start here."

—**MATT DEFINA**, Organisational Psychologist and
Head of Programs & Impact at The Man Cave

"Dr. Tony Daloisio has done it! He has written the comprehensive guide for men to find joy, passion, and purpose in life. *The Journeyman Life* offers a very practical guide for all men to be introspective, honest, and thoughtful with effective change, continuous improvement, and the ability to define one's highest level of meaning in a whole-person way. Above all, Tony's book will connect you with how to be the best version of yourself—authentic, resilient, and purposeful. This is a must-read for anyone who is open to change and transformation both personally and professionally."

—**MICHAEL K. SIMPSON**, Amazon #1 bestselling author
in Executive Coaching and author of *Unlocking Potential* and
Powerful Leadership through Coaching

"With refreshing vulnerability, Tony invites us to take up the wild, heartbreaking, and exhilarating journey of life. He reminds us of the transformational wisdom that so many of us men need to hear—that we are both perfectly imperfect just as we are and that we can grow into so much more. Tony reminds us that life's breakdowns provide the most reliable breakthroughs if we are willing to go on an inner journey. This is an important book for those who long to create the brave, wise, and compassionate world that so many men dream of."

—**DR. BRANDON NAPPI**, Founder of Copper Beech Institute

"Believing in your own ability to transform and grow is always critical, regardless of your age. Tony reminds us that vulnerability and embracing your imperfections is important for everyone."

—**CHIP CONLEY**, Founder of Modern Elder Academy

"Tony has always been a seeker and a catalyst for other seekers. He is a true Journeyman, and in this book, he takes us on a compelling journey—from the inside out. Integrating a wealth of experience, both personally and professionally, with the latest research on 'what makes men tick,' he offers a roadmap for any man seeking to up his game in this thing we call a well-lived life. *The Journeyman Life* is a major contribution to the field of adult-male development. Do yourself a favor and read and follow the wise and practical counsel in this book."

—**DR. NEIL YEAGER**, author of *The Seventh Prism*,
The Leader's Window, and the best-selling *Power Interviews*

"Try as we might, no man escapes a quiet voice that asks, 'Who am I?' and 'What do I really want in this life?' Time passes, and the reality of age subtly turns up the volume on that internal chatter, and yet even in later years, lifelong questions frequently remain unanswered because it takes being vulnerable and risks losing the protection we have unwittingly amassed. Tony's journey, captured here, is both a testament to his own pursuit of truth and nothing less than an extraordinary gift to men."

—**WILLIAM SPEAR**, Founder and CEO of Fortunate
Blessings Foundation and Higher Education Consultant

"Do you want to let life carry you along passively, or do you want to grab an oar and learn to steer and propel yourself? Tony Daloisio is a wise and practical guide, and *The Journeyman Life* is the guidebook to learning to live actively rather than passively. I'm so grateful to have found it before more of life passed, and I urge you to read it today."

—**PETER BECKER**, Head of School at the Frederick Gunn School

"A daring look at a subject many have shied away from because it requires truth seeking, truth telling, reflection, and individual change. We have an obligation to ourselves, our relationships, and our purpose on earth to be better by increasing our capacity mentally, emotionally, physically, and spiritually in order to be more, do more, and serve more. And when we do, our little corner of the world becomes a better place. But holding up a mirror or a capacity gauge takes courage and fortitude to make the journey to a better life . . . a journeyman life."

—**KENDALL LYMAN**, Principal at The Highlands Group and author *of Change the Way You Change*

"Being a man today can be challenging and lonely. Yet through his journey of vulnerability and trust, Tony shows us a path of not only feeling more alive and connected to each other, but maybe, most importantly, to ourselves."

—**PETER CALLAHAN**, Leadership & Engagement Director at Copper Beech Institute

"Tony's work has been revolutionary for myself and for the team of directors at Skellig. Tony's realness and tenacity to boldly get to the issues and then guide safely to a resolution is profound. I'm glad I met Tony, and working with him has led to many moments of truth."

—**PAUL O'SULLIVAN**, CEO and Founder of Skellig

THE NOT-SO-PERFECT
PATH *to a* LIFE WELL LIVED

THE
JOURNEYMAN
LIFE

TONY C. DALOISIO, PhD

RIVER GROVE
BOOKS

Published by River Grove Books
Austin, TX
www.rivergrovebooks.com

Distributed by River Grove Books

Design and composition by Greenleaf Book Group
Cover design by Greenleaf Book Group
Image: Man alone on foggy road; Back view of walking man, used under license from Shutterstock.com

Publisher's Cataloging-in-Publication data is available.

Print ISBN: 978-1-63299-474-5

eBook ISBN: 978-1-63299-475-2

First Edition

This book is about the work of my life, both personal and professional. I decided to write it to offer up the learning I have had and to share with others the mission that I have chosen: to improve my life and the lives of others. I also wanted to share my innermost thoughts and experiences with my grandchildren, the next generation to better the world. I studied in the field of psychology and have been a practicing organizational and personal psychologist and university professor and researcher for over thirty years.

The book is aimed squarely at and for men who seek to improve their lives, and it is primarily dedicated to those men who wish to evolve and change the traditional role of men in our society. Men who wish to improve the quality of their relationships with significant others, families, children, and professional associates. The work is not easy, but it is extremely important and rewarding. I have been and still am in the process of applying the ideas in this book to better myself. That is the journey of a man in hopes of a life well lived.

CONTENTS

INTRODUCTION

T his book is about you, who you have become and who you want to become. It is about your outer self—the self that interacts with the world, and your inner self—the feelings, core issues, and hopes that are the driving forces for the decisions you make in the outer world that ultimately become the person you are in life. That is what I am calling the story of you. In essence, it is the journey of you, a man in our society, the not-so-perfect path that we all take in life. The most critical question is not so much who you have become but who you can, want to, and will become in your quest for a life well lived.

This book is also about me and the story of me, the writer, as I have been actively reflecting on that journey for myself my entire life. I have also taken on the challenge to help myself and others understand how to navigate that journey more effectively. To that end, I will share parts of my inner journey and the outer journey with you to bring this to life. I am pretty sure that you will relate strongly to my stories and challenges and that you have a similar version yourself. Likely, we are more the same as men than we are different. The path that got us here and the path that will take us to a better place are the same.

It is likely, during or after reading this book, that you will be faced with a decision that I was faced with years ago and in many ways continue to face each day of my life. It is a decision and challenge so profound and potentially impactful that I call it the hardest choice I have had to make, the toughest set of factors that I have had to endure: the decision to come to grips with my outer self and work on my inner self.

You might be questioning that statement. Let me explain. It wasn't the pain I endured as the child of an obsessive-compulsive, neurotic mother whose two other boys passed away, leaving me to be the obsessed-upon boy left in her life. It wasn't the mental and physical abuse that I endured being locked in the house with her for fear that something would happen to me. It wasn't watching the torture she subjected my dad to; he was fearful of leaving her to have her way with me and my sister, Dolores. It wasn't the humiliation and embarrassment that I felt as a child because of her outrageous behavior. It wasn't that I didn't start to find my voice and self until my mid-twenties, or the immense challenge I endured to overachieve and attain a PhD in psychology in a futile attempt to preempt the mental illness that her psychiatrist told her I would have because of her. It wasn't the decision to leave my corner office and executive role to venture out from scratch and start my own business, which was terrifying! It wasn't looking myself squarely in the face and realizing that because of my unresolved core issues in life I had lost my first marriage of eighteen years. It wasn't the shame I felt having to share with the kids that we were getting divorced, or feeling like I was not a good father to my teenage son, Timothy, and our six-year-old daughter, Morgan. It wasn't the oncologist sharing a stage-3 bladder cancer diagnosis, the ensuing chemotherapy, and multiple surgeries that took me out of my life and career for two years. It wasn't taking on a challenging role as a professor in the business school at Georgia Tech.

These things were incredibly hard but not as challenging as realizing well into my second marriage that I was experiencing the same feelings and challenges I had in my first marriage, and realizing that the adage "Wherever I go, there I am" might be applicable to me. I was on the brink of losing love once again. I was even able to entertain the fact that I wasn't the person I thought I was or hoped to be, and that people were seeing through me, seeing and experiencing the inner turmoil that I was feeling myself my entire life.

It was about that time that I had to come face-to-face with myself to ask that most difficult question I raised previously: Was I courageous enough to take on the core inner issues that have been driving my outer life challenges my entire life? I originally faced that challenge twenty-nine years ago when Teresa and I met, and I decided to work hard to improve myself from the inside out. I made great progress, but plenty of issues remained. Two years ago, when I decided to begin seriously researching and writing this book, the real work began.

To me, living with integrity means coming to grips with oneself regarding the gap that exists between who you aspire to be and who you are. It is much easier to narrow this gap in your mind when you are not challenging yourself, not opening up to feedback from others and deeply looking at yourself from the inside and outside. The adage that comes to mind is, "We judge ourselves by our intentions and others by their behaviors." Indeed, one of the greatest motivators in life is that of self-preservation.

For me the gap clearly existed. My focus on the persona I spent my entire life perfectly crafting got in the way of true change and growth. I was stubborn and defensive and clearly very invested in preserving and building my ego and in maintaining my self-image. This was a response to that core issue in the pit of my stomach telling me that I didn't have a voice, that my ideas did not matter, and that I needed to go it alone, independent of others—which I believed was the only way to be truly safe and secure as a man. Those feelings drove my thoughts, behaviors, and actions at most every juncture of my life.

If I take the other side of the story of me, I can readily see the anger, frustration, protection, aggression, and fear that was eating me up inside and driving those less effective behaviors and thoughts about my roles in life as a father, husband, leader, son, athlete, and friend. I can see the impact of those energies that inhabited my body and mind and the resultant hurtful and ineffective strategies I took to control outcomes and keep my ego intact.

The big challenge is taking yourself on in that battle to overcome yourself, and breaking the habit of being yourself. You must take this challenge on seriously, methodically, honestly, and with a true beginner's mind.

What you will become is what is at stake. The decision to take yourself on may be the most important decision of your life, and it will likely be the hardest work of your life. Hopefully, it will also be the most rewarding journey you will ever take.

Though its actual origins are unknown, Socrates is often attributed with the quote, "The beginning of wisdom is the definition of terms." The truth of this aphorism is self-evident, regardless of who said it. Let us begin with some terms that I used in the title of the book and which are at the core of this book's premise and the work you will do:

· A well-lived life

· Not-so-perfect path

· The journey of a man

Please note that I will frame each from my perspective and attempt to give you a chance to add your thoughts into the definition for yourself and how you might apply it to your journey.

A Well-Lived Life

Clearly there are lots of ways to define what is meant by "a well-lived life." It is an existential question we as human beings routinely ask ourselves, and one that has been studied by many philosophers, psychologists, and economists. Some see a well-lived life as a life of happiness, as professor Laurie Santos suggests in her course on happiness at Yale, which was voted the most valuable and highest rated in the school's storied history. But as Nobel Prize–winner in economics Daniel Kahneman suggests, happiness or even high-ground moral character are not the be-all and end-all prize in life. He suggests that it is the degree to which we transcend ourselves as Maslow postulated in the later years of his life as one of the preeminent psychologists of the last century. Perhaps it is our empathy and compassion for others that describes living life well.

When I ask myself this question, I think of a few things. Am I a good person? Do I treat others with respect and kindness? Am I a loving father, husband, son, friend, and community member? Am I giving back to the world based on my superpowers and my strengths? Am I at peace with myself, and do I have self-respect? Am I growing and learning and striving to get better in my life? Do I have compassion for others and even myself? Lastly, am I living my values, in my integrity?

The list goes on for sure, and I believe the most important thing is for you to come up with your definition for yourself. You can be as expansive as you wish. After all, it's your definition that is important.

Another interesting piece of research I came across was Harvard Medical School's Harvard Grant Study, one of the longest-running longitudinal research studies in history. For seventy years, it has tracked hundreds of men, graduates from Harvard Medical School, Business School, and Law School as well as a parallel group from the Boston area that were more diverse in ethnic, socioeconomic, and other factors. The study was conducted to help discover the important factors that helped determine life success and well-being for these men.

One might expect that professional success, intelligence, and degrees were the most important variables. However, the study found that the most important variable that contributed to a man's well-being, health, and vibrancy in life was the quality of the relationships that he had with others. It was a stunning finding. The questions that emerge for me are these: What is a quality relationship? What is the impact of that on one's life success?

Perhaps you could think about your answer to those two important questions. Here are some of my thoughts and ideas that have emerged from the research studies: A quality relationship is one where there is depth, honesty, vulnerability, respect, openness, and compassion or empathy for the other. In addition, we could throw in a good dose of fun and mutual interests. We have a sound emotional bank account with the other, and we are close to each other and have an influence in each other's lives. Looking at the impact of this on well-being, we can note a few things that contribute. Humans are deep down and genetically disposed to being social creatures. We live together in society to support each other, work together for the common good, complement each other, help each other, and ultimately love each other. Those elements are strongly correlated with the concept of well-being in the literature. There are many stories of men who had been married for over sixty years and when the wife passes, the husband passes within a short period of time from a broken heart. But when we look more closely, we see that fundamental psychological and emotional well-being—and likely the ensuing chemicals that are stimulated by these relationships—are critical to one's continuing life force and without it, we perish.

The task of defining a well-lived life is somewhat of an inside job and an outside job. The outside part is the fact that we often judge ourselves as compared to others on the ladder of success and happiness without examining what is truly meaningful and important to our most personal mission in life. I would contend that for men—and I know it is true for me—we are singularly focused on achieving our goals. This is a more straight-lined and singularly focused approach to life. But in reality, I know that a well-lived life is much more than that and the Harvard Grant Study mentioned previously certainly gives me—and I would imagine you—a bit of pause in the consideration of the question, What is a well-lived life?

The inside aspect of this question is one for each of us to reconcile in our lives. The important part of this consideration for me and hopefully for you is that we do stop at some point and look at ourselves and the world we have built and take time to seriously consider the question and the answer to that question. For you and me, this book and the process it takes you through on your journey is a guide that will allow us to look at our lives from the inside to craft a current and meaningful answer to that question. It is only with that perspective that we will find the ultimate motivation to go on this journey to look, change, develop, and fulfill those aspects that will bring us closer to the goal of a well-lived life as we look at it from the end looking back.

The Not-So-Perfect Path

Conceiving of this book was the most profound, interesting, scary, and likely fruitful aspect of both putting myself on the examination table and deeply looking at what I would have to do to get my life in alignment with my values and vision. In the past twenty-plus years, it has become very clear to me that my path was not a straight line—more likely lots of twists and turns, successes, and failures. You likely have noticed in your life as well that it is difficult to hold all the aspects of life in check and make it all happen just as you'd hoped. As if that isn't hard enough, it became clearer to me that unless I took time to reflect on my path, my goal, my values, and my relationships, it was likely that I would end up off course. The perfectionist voice inside me didn't want to accept the idea that I could not control the path of my life and also that experiencing failure was an important part of life. Anything less than outstanding success and accolades to boost my otherwise fragile ego took me down, made me angry, made me blame others, and propelled me to buckle up and work harder. It seemed like there was no room in that equation for "not perfect." Having a growth mindset and an openness to learning, and accepting that life is about trial and error is way more appropriate and practical. In this book, the phrase "not perfect" means that we are all on this seemingly imperfect yet very perfect journey called life. When we are unconscious and not open to events, we fight the wave, and the wave usually wins. When we are more present and conscious in this journey we can learn and grow from the things that come our way. I am learning to be more accepting of these events and lean into them as gifts. How about you?

The Journey of a Man

The third piece of the puzzle, "the journey of a man," or journeyman, was originally written about and researched by the noted sociologist Joseph Campbell in his book *The Hero's Journey*. In this narratology, the hero goes on an adventure, is victorious in a decisive crisis, and comes home a changed or transformed man. We are reminded of the call to adventure, the abyss, the revelations, the atonement, the transformation, and the return in this mythical journey. It is usually about overcoming temptations and bringing oneself to the threshold of the new world. In the following pages, you and I will embark on this epic journey.

As we continue the context setting for our journey and the story of you, a few more pieces of the puzzle might be useful as lenses through which to view your life. The first is the notion of true effectiveness, the ability to get results in life while cultivating our capability to be healthy, happy, in relationships that are of high quality, and taking care of our inner and outer lives. I learned one approach to calibrating this measure from my close ten-year partnership with Stephen R. Covey and the Covey Leadership Center. In his epic worldwide blockbuster bestseller *The 7 Habits of Highly Effective People*, he takes on this issue by sharing the Aesop fable of the farmer and the goose that produced golden eggs. The farmer becomes short-sighted and kills the goose in an effort to harvest all the eggs and in the process kills the capability of producing the eggs. Our lives are a bit like that, especially as men, as we take little time to cultivate our well-being and capability while overemphasizing the achievement, output, or production side of the existential dilemma of life. I know for me over the years, I had the feeling that I was bullet proof and could keep on going like the Energizer Bunny. This approach to well-being and life is too shortsighted and doesn't work in the long run.

As we begin the process of looking at ourselves—at our truths, hopes, and dreams—we would do well to remember and apply a framework that I learned about from Dr. Harvell Hendricks: the notion of the different types of truth available to us in self-reflection and relationships. The second piece of the puzzle is to think about this as you examine your truths about yourself in the story of you.

The first truth is the *false truth,* which is a one-sided story, vilifying others, placing the blame on the other and absolving oneself as a victim of one's childhood, bad luck, or other people. This is false as it is told from a reactive mindset, taking little or no responsibility for one's actions.

The second truth is a *half-truth,* which is taking some measure of responsibility for happenings in one's life but generalizing about them and hiding out in that superficial story. I might say to myself, "I am reluctant to be vulnerable with others because my father was that way, and it is my personality." That is a half-truth. Missing are important details of how this belief is alive in me today, how I might change that, why it doesn't work for me at this point in my life, etc. It is like we are going through the motions to share our story and leaving out the most important voices and characters and taking little responsibility for this story.

The third truth is called *microscopic truth.* This is giving data about what sensations you are feeling in the moment. It's expressing your internal experience as you are perceiving it at this time, proving that intimacy is really "into me you see." It's speaking from your heart, honoring your needs, and speaking your truth to break through the layers of protection and get to the truth that is undeniable, beyond the realm of blame, judgment, and defense—the truth of your soul! This is the level of honesty, clarity, and accuracy that is needed in your life reflection. You need this level of microscopic truth to craft the story of you.

Regarding your journey to a well-lived life, there is indeed much at stake—for you, your family, our communities, and the world. The path is before us, and the choice to enter that path is yours to make. I sincerely hope you make that choice and join me and thousands of men on this journey. It is said that every epic journey begins with one step. Let that one step be your choice to not only read this book, but to also embrace the challenges and opportunities that will emerge for you in that embrace.

CHAPTER 1

THE STORY OF YOU

Because I was not comfortable with who I had become, and because I have always been a seeker, wanting to learn, grow, and be a better and more effective person, I decided to more deeply examine my life and the lives of how men operated in our society. I was ultimately looking for answers and guidance for improving my life, but I also wanted to help other men do the same. As I began examining my life, it became clear that there were likely several angles to pursue, several lenses to look through and degrees of honesty and reality that I would have to sift through to tell an accurate story of who I had become. You will likely find the same is true for you. In the process, I was talking with my friend Barbara Vacarr, a former executive director of Kripalu Center for Yoga & Health in Stockbridge, Massachusetts, about this notion. She shared the following framework with me and thought it would work well in describing this aspect of the journey of a man. There are three stories in each of us: our personal story, the hidden self, and the unknown self.

Your Personal Story

The first story is the story of how you hope to be seen in the world. Most of us spend our lifetime crafting and cultivating our persona. It is likely composed of a view of our personality that is aspirational, positive, self-oriented, and perhaps more forgiving of our weaknesses. Self-preservation is a very strong drive that guides our behavior and our view of ourselves. We are probably quite invested in our persona and likely quite defensive about it as well. It's OK for you to poke holes in it, but it's not so OK for others to do so.

While I have spent hundreds if not thousands of hours coaching leaders and have participated in as many persona conversations, the persona that I know best and am going to share with you as an example is my own, of myself. It will also be useful for you to see the progression and relationship among the three stories of me. I hope that in doing so you'll better be able to map your three stories as well. Your stories will help you uncover your insights and closely held beliefs about yourself and ultimately help you get greater clarity about the story of you.

As I write this, I notice that who I am and who I want to be in the outer world are at odds to some extent. The persona I project is one of a strong, confident, independent, thoughtful, and kind person. I'm a bit guarded for sure, but because of my education and training and my profession as a psychologist, I tend to want to go deep with folks, to ask provocative questions, and to be transparent about my own awareness and distinctions about life and relationships. I enjoy that process and connection. I believe that I want to be seen as someone with depth and of substance, as this has been a drive of mine for as long as I can recall, largely in response to the big hole in my soul around my own self-image. Often the core issue that we struggle with in our life story is a main character in our persona that strives to compensate for the challenge we see in ourselves.

In order to discover this gap or hole in your soul and its implications in your life, you need to dig deeper into this persona as it is often not aligned with your values or true intentions.

To help you discover more about your persona, here are a few things you can do:

- Question your motivation in taking actions or making decisions.

- Ask others how they see you. If you are lucky, someone who cares a great deal for you will share the truth lovingly, and you will benefit greatly. My brother-in-law, Rex, did that for me many years ago. While I was surprised at what he said, it made perfect sense given what I know about my persona.

- Ask what is important to you inside yourself and also as relates to how others see you. An example for me is that I want to be seen as competent and professional and having my stuff together. I like that I am a psychologist and get to help others with their problems; it kind of gets me off the hook in dealing with my own challenges.

- Begin to explore deeper the real you, your wants, needs, hopes, and what is truly important to you.

The Hidden Self

The second story we tell about ourselves or could tell is that of the hidden self, the private self. This represents the inner drives, motives, aspirations, fears, beliefs, and image of your true self. It would be like if you pulled back the curtain, like in *The Wizard of Oz,* and we finally got to see the true nature of the all-powerful wizard. We see his real story, his rawer emotions, fears, and workarounds.

For me, looking inside at this part of myself for that story has been difficult and scary. I have worked very hard to create the outer façade of myself—having it all together and being a leader and helper of others. In a way, this has shielded me from having to deal with my own stuff, and it keeps me safe. Questions to ask include these:

- What consumes your thinking, what do you obsess about, what do you fear and work hard to overcome?

- What are the core issues that have traveled the world and the years of your life with you, like an uninvited guest that keeps showing up in your life?

- What is it that you are hiding from others about yourself?

- What might happen if your true inner self were uncovered and shared with your loved ones, friends, and professional associates?

The Unknown Self

The third story is the story of the undiscovered you, perhaps the aspirational you, the possible you. This story is unknown to you and others and is perhaps the most important story and the most exciting one. It is the you that is likely the resolution of the first two stories. It is the one that can change your life's trajectory.

For me, as I sat with myself in deliberation and preparation for writing this book, exploring my third story, I had to determine if I would take on this vision of my potential life or settle for the safer ground of story one while keeping story two hidden as much as possible. I have decided to go for it, but I waiver often, and I believe that is the nature of the third story. All we can do is bring it to awareness and begin to live into it and share it with others in a courageous and honest manner. While I am doing that in this book and in my life now, I still find myself with one foot in story one and often stuck in story two.

The real purpose of the three stories is to step back from your day-to-day life, take an honest look at yourself, and determine what story is driving your life and whether you want to change it.

There are two additional perspectives or frames of reference that I would like to share with you that have been a great help to me as a lens to see myself and my story and to give me hope: the archetypes of male behavior and the stages of adult development.

Archetypes of the Masculine Psyche

The first lens is based on the work of turn-of-the-century renowned psychologist Carl Jung. He postulated that there are four archetypes of the masculine psyche. A masculine archetype is a sociological or psychological construct that suggests there are clusters or behavior patterns that show up in men. As we are all wired in similar ways biologically, we have similar themes instilled in us via our society, and we are driven to play out specific roles in our system of living. While these do vary by tribe, country, nationality, and even time period, Jung suggested that they stand the test of time and cross sociological and other barriers. This is a powerful notion, and I believe a helpful one.

As you read about the four archetypes of the masculine psyche, I suggest you try to discern which one is the most dominant in describing your typical behavior patterns. All men use each of the four patterns, but we each have one or two of the four that are most like us. The unique version of our own archetype is formed—likely in childhood—based on family dynamics, or a version could evolve out of our DNA, a natural disposition that we have toward one or the other.

The other element of the archetypes that is important to consider is that each has a mostly positive manifestation of that style, called the mature masculine, and also a shadow or misused aspect of that same archetype. After the description of the four, I will share with you my own version of the psyche that is uniquely mine and give you some sense of how I know that and where it likely came from and how it serves or doesn't serve me in my life. Hopefully you can do the same for yourself after reading this section. These are the biological, physiological, and psychological markers for males over the centuries, if not from the time of the caveman.

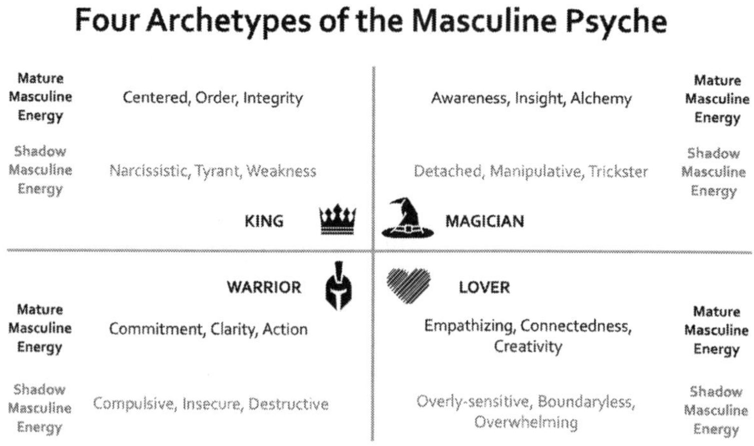

Four Archetypes of the Masculine Psyche

Mature Masculine Energy	Centered, Order, Integrity		Awareness, Insight, Alchemy	Mature Masculine Energy
Shadow Masculine Energy	Narcissistic, Tyrant, Weakness		Detached, Manipulative, Trickster	Shadow Masculine Energy
	KING 👑	🎩 MAGICIAN		
	WARRIOR ⚔	♥ LOVER		
Mature Masculine Energy	Commitment, Clarity, Action		Empathizing, Connectedness, Creativity	Mature Masculine Energy
Shadow Masculine Energy	Compulsive, Insecure, Destructive		Overly-sensitive, Boundaryless, Overwhelming	Shadow Masculine Energy

Figure 1.1

18

THE KING

The first archetype of the masculine psyche is called *the king*. It represents the wise, integrous, stabilizing, and noble aspect of the mature masculine. King energy is centered, has a deep knowing, and is calm and bestowing on others, much like a king would be if he were leading his kingdom in a mature, loving, and positive manner. Think of a leader who you have admired in history or in current life or a role model you had, perhaps even your father or a loving grandparent. We each have king energy in us and strive to use it wisely and often in our world.

The shadow side of the king is the tyrant. He exploits and abuses out of self-interest and fear. He is often narcissistic, aggressive, and willing to misuse his power out of that weakness. Instead of caring for others, he gives away his positive power, rendering only his authority. This behavior comes from a place of weakness and low self-esteem. A good example of this is King Herod in the time of Jesus. As he learns that Jesus is born, his power is threatened, and he decrees that all male babies in Jerusalem be killed.

Where in you do you see the king archetype, either the mature version or the shadow version? For me, I know that I have misused my strengths and power to feed my ego in the name of gaining advantage over others. I also have been able to use my natural energy to lead groups in positive directions in lots of different situations. Certainly, in my later years, I am coming more into my mature king style as I settle into the peace of the golden years.

THE WARRIOR

The warrior is the second archetype of the masculine psyche. The mature version of the warrior archetype reaches out and fights for what he wants. This archetype has a clear sense of the results that are wanted and the direction that one should take. It is courageous and confident in taking that path. The warrior knows what he wants, and he knows how to get it. He is alert and clear and realizes that every action counts and that any hesitation may result in failure. The warrior has the skill, power, motivation, and energy to achieve the results he desires. A good example of the warrior archetype is someone like Churchill, who was able to respond courageously to a very difficult situation that faced England during World War II.

The shadow side of the warrior archetype is the emotionally distant, detached man. He will endure any pain, attack anyone, work beyond his limits, and can often be cruel and dispassionate of others.

I know this archetype very well as this is my strongest identity. On the positive side, I'm willing to do most anything to achieve results that I desire, even if it makes me uncomfortable. This energy has driven me a great deal in my life to do things in some ways that others might have thought beyond my capability. On the shadow side for me, my warrior sometimes will do things at the expense of other people. I can think of situations where I used my strength and willpower and skills to overpower someone who I perceived as an enemy or whom I desired to win over or win out. I'm not proud to share that with you, but it is my reality I'm afraid.

Consider the aspects of yourself where the warrior lives, both the mature side and the shadow side. Then you might consider how strong this particular archetype is in your DNA and in the path that you choose to follow in the world.

THE MAGICIAN

The third architect of the masculine psyche is the magician. The mature version of the magician is the man who has incredible insight and is able to see deep into the mysteries of life and relationships. It is the force in the *Star Wars* movie represented by Obi-Wan Kenobi. It is Merlin in the King Arthur stories. These magicians are able to see behind the human dynamics to how the universe works, and then channel their power toward either good or evil. Some might consider Einstein or Yoda from the magician archetype.

The shadow side of the magician archetype is that of being secretive, being manipulative, hiding motives, fooling people, and taking advantage of others. The dark magician comes across as the innocent one but is really not so innocent. One of my friends spent most of his time—and I'm sure you know a person like this—trying to be funny, sometimes at the expense of others but mostly to be clever. To some extent, everyone loves the comedian, but like anything else, when it's overdone, it's not so funny. It could be debilitating to that person and to others.

Think about the magician archetype and what aspects of your own personality are alive in this element, both the mature version and the shadow version.

THE LOVER

The last of the archetypes is the lover. In the positive version of this archetype, the male is extremely sensitive to the world, connected to others, full of life, attuned to aesthetics. He has the ability to read people. The lover is quite creative and is often seen as an artist. He often operates based on hunches and is very spontaneous.

The shadow side of the lover is more about longing, detachment, delaying gratification, and feeling depressed.

One of the things I think of when I think of this archetype is the character of Dan played by Steve Carell in the movie *Dan in Real*

Life. At the beginning of the movie, he was in his shadow archetype of the lover, but then he met his real love, and suddenly he came alive and the fires of life were ignited inside of him.

WHICH ARCHETYPE IS MOST YOU?

Carl Jung's archetypes of the masculine psyche provide a very interesting lens through which to look at yourself in the story of you, offering additional perspectives for you to evaluate whether you are operating from the mature version of an archetype or the immature or shadow side of that type.

It's most likely that, like me, you have one archetype that is your sort of go-to style, and that style generally evolves from some core issue that lies deep in your inner self. For me, the warrior looms large, primarily because I had no voice in the family dynamic I grew up in. I was dominated by a powerful mother, and the only way for me to have any sense of myself was to be a warrior, to fight for my own voice, and to fight for the things that I desired in my life. I learned that lesson early, but I know that I have tipped the scale often toward the shadow side of the warrior. It has also served me greatly, as I have achieved many goals in my life because of my ability to face my fears and my willingness to compete and go beyond my own comfort zone.

The Stages of Adult Development

Learning about the stages of adult development gave me great perspective on knowing myself and what actions I needed to take to improve and get to the next level. I'm hoping you will find my research useful as well.

Dr. Robert Kegan, a Harvard psychologist, has been the preeminent researcher in this field. I had the opportunity to meet him and study with him a few years ago. In a nutshell, developing as an adult is not about learning new things, adding things to the container of the mind. It is about personal transformation, changing the manner in which we know and view the world. Instead of changing the contents of the mind, it is akin to changing the actual container.

That transformation is metaphorically a Copernican shift, realizing that the Earth is—or you are—not at the center of our solar system, but the sun is at the center. When we realize this, nothing really changes, but rather our entire conception and perception of the world transforms.

We experience this often in life. I remember moving back to a town I'd lived in earlier in life and found the people to be so much more friendly. But I was the one who had changed! Only through transformation can we truly move from one stage of human development to a higher stage. Often a personal tragedy is powerful enough to signal the growth in perspective to be a catalyst for this step change.

For me, I have had several such shifts in perspective that have had a profound influence on how I saw the world and what I did as a result. The birth of my child, divorce, cancer, and retirement were some of the most significant events that changed my perspective and still affect how I see the world to this day.

Stage 1 of Kegan's development is the impulsive mind. This is early childhood. Stage 2 is the imperial mind, which is our adolescence. Around 6 percent of the population is in this stage. Stage 3 is the socialized mind, which represents 58 percent of the adult population. Stage 4 is the self-authoring mind, and around 35 percent of the population is in this stage. Finally, stage 5 is the self-transforming mind, which only about 1 percent of us reach.

STAGE 2: THE IMPERIAL MIND

Let's pick up at stage 2, as it is most relevant to our purpose. Most of the time, we are in transition between stages, and we behave a bit differently with different people in our lives. The goal is to know where we are, what behavior looks like at that stage, where it comes from, and how it is serving us and others—the impact. When we know those elements, and we have motivation, clarity, and focus, we can deliberately work to change ourselves at the belief, thought, and feeling levels.

This stage is about getting your own needs met, as opposed to a shared internal experience with others. The fear is that your own needs will not be met. Additionally, at this stage, you follow rules not because of the goodness of the rule but because doing so will benefit you. Typically, teens and young adults are at this stage of development.

STAGE 3: THE SOCIALIZED MIND

The vast majority of us are at this stage, which is a bit amazing and scary. But it also makes sense as one thinks about the behavior patterns of most adults.

The most important things in stage 2 were our personal needs and interests. In stage 3, the most important things are the ideas, norms, and beliefs of people in systems around us—for example, our family, society, or culture and ideology. We begin to function based more on how others experience us. For example, we take an external view of ourselves: We might tell ourselves, *They'll think I look stupid* or might even internalize that and think that we *are* actually stupid.

In this stage, we tend to arrive at our beliefs and even morals from external sources. Those could be religion, work, culture, or friends. Additionally, in this stage, we give a great deal of responsibility to other people in terms of how they see us, so that we spend most of our time trying to avoid looking bad or hurting other people's feelings. We tend to look for validation about our own self-worth from outside of ourselves. We also tend to internalize others' perspectives and actually care more about their opinions than what is right and wrong.

One of the reasons a person in stage 3 of adult development would feel guilty about having an affair, for example, is that it would be disturbing. The dissonance comes from the feeling that cheating is wrong and goes against one's beliefs and values. In stage 3, the self-talk would be "I am in relationships, and I follow the rules in order to fit in."

I was able to be a part of a research study that tested the stage of development one was in. I was surprised to see that I was mostly in stage 3. I find my focus is, to a great extent, outside of myself, even though I have great independence and strong opinions. It seems more to keep me safe in relation to others. I often make decisions in response or reaction to others. I know this sounds quite wimpy, and I am not suggesting I don't have opinions or beliefs or that I don't work hard to center on my values. But I am very bound by this seeming need for approval or self-image reinforcement. It is a great realization, and I am always working hard to change it.

What about you? Does this stage of development sound like you? It is what I will spend a great deal of time in the next two chapters describing as the reactive mindset—that is, making decisions in reaction to a situation as opposed to making them based on well-thought-out values and principles in your life. I know it is a subtle distinction, but it is an important one.

STAGE 4: THE SELF-AUTHORING MIND

According to Kegan, about 35 percent of adults are in this stage of development. In stage 4, we put the priority on defining who we are, and we move away from being defined by other people, our relationships, or the environment. We believe that we are an individual with thoughts, beliefs, and feelings, and that we are independent from the expectations of our culture. In this stage, we're able to differentiate the opinions of others from our own, and we develop what Kegan calls our "seat of judgment": *This is the person I am, and this is what I stand for.* In this stage, we develop an internal sense of direction and the capacity to develop and follow our own charted course. Additional characteristics include the ability to question our own expectations and beliefs, to hold strong to what we believe, to define limits, and to solve problems with a strong sense of right and wrong for ourselves. In a sense, in stage 4, we have self-authored our own beliefs.

I have thought about the notion that at some point in life we look inside at our values and prioritize them over the ego drive to take care of ourselves at the expense of our values. One of the most difficult things for me growing up in my family dynamic was that I did not have a voice. That lack of a voice stayed with me well into my late twenties. It was only during graduate school that I really developed my voice after reading some amazing books like *Man's Search for Meaning* by Viktor Frankl. Another book that had a huge impact on me was Carl Rogers's *On Becoming a Person.*

In this stage, we also take responsibility for our own emotions. We're clear about what our feelings are, and we attempt to self-regulate those feelings. We gain a better understanding of our outer world and are able to see things from others' perspectives. We learn that we can change and grow and still be safe and that it is worth it to do so.

Self-authorship is about defining and reshaping what you believe, your sense of inner self, and your means of relating to others rather than uncritically accepting those ideas from other people or from a place of fear. All three of these dimensions are critical for the construction of a stage 4 set of actions. We would need to generate our own values. We would need to have a strong adherence to integrity. Finally, we will be thinking a great deal about the feelings and relationships of others rather than being subject to them and moving out of fear. The key to stage 4 is to view yourself as the object, something that can be evaluated, analyzed, and understood.

STAGE 5: THE INTERCONNECTED MIND

Only 1 percent of adults from the research studies are operating at stage 5. In stage 5, your sense of self is not tethered to specific identities or roles. Rather, it is regularly created through the exploration of your own identity. It is cultivated through interaction with others. In this sense, the self is ever evolving, in a constant state of change.

In this stage, we not only question authority, but we also question ourselves. We recognize the complexities of life, and we're constantly reinventing our own identity. Another important component of this stage is that we can hold multiple thoughts and ideologies at once; we can balance and honor those perspectives simultaneously.

A good example of this is when you find yourself disagreeing with someone about a really important issue. In stage 5, you can look at the situation more objectively and truly understand both perspectives in an effort to explore them deeply. You can then use the data from that analysis to be able to come up with sort of a third alternative, more of a win-win solution. This is very hard to do, especially when you have strong beliefs or when you feel challenged.

THE CATERPILLAR

In conclusion, Kegan's adult development stages lay out a clear path for how we want to show up in the world. Do we want to follow other people's expectations for us or forge our own way? Do we want to be trapped by old patterns of thinking, or do we want to develop new ways of being for ourselves? Do we want to just get by in our relationships, or do we want to cultivate deeper, more authentic relationships with other people in our lives?

Where do you think you are, according to Kegan? We all believe we're in a higher stage than we are. To get a realistic understanding of your own stage, it's important to pay attention to how you behave across many different situations with many different people. Development is critical as we grow older and as life becomes more complicated. It's very difficult to move through the stages and thrive. We constantly need new ways of thinking about ourselves in the world.

I have struggled with this notion and have found that having a purpose, a project, a set of goals, a continued awareness, and most importantly, feedback and openness to that feedback allows me to continue to evolve and grow into the next stages of development. I find the exciting thing here is that we don't stop growing and learning in our twenties; we continue to evolve if we are motivated to do so. Kegan's analogy of the caterpillar gives us that hope as we see hundreds of such examples of this change and evolution in nature. Like a caterpillar, we have the potential to transform into butterflies— that is, to reach a higher level of development and consciousness. A caterpillar does not die as a caterpillar. A caterpillar transforms into a butterfly.

Development isn't inevitable, and Kegan found that most adults don't experience meaningful growth. The key question becomes how we can keep developing and growing as we get older. We need to change both how we think about the world and what we think about it. It's not just accumulating more knowledge; it's about changing our perspective. We do this by continually questioning our hidden assumptions and beliefs.

Psychological and Emotional Safety

In a relationship, there are a couple of different important factors that allow you to flourish and grow and transform from one stage to the other. One of them is the concept of psychological and emotional safety. This is when you consider your relationship a safe place where you can fully express what you're thinking and feeling without feeling judged. It involves sharing hard, painful, and uncomfortable thoughts without being afraid of the response. This type of safety allows us to grow, because it requires us to be vulnerable, owning our own stories, which can often be very uncomfortable.

Jack Mezirow, the founder of transformation learning theory, calls it *rational discourse:* having an active dialogue with others to better understand the meaning of our experience. This is really important because it allows us to think critically and deeply and to have an authentic and clear conversation with other people, which is critical to development. The most important component here is a discourse, a dialogue that allows us to state our thoughts and engage others so that we can, in a sense, reflect our ideas off one another. When we can open ourselves up to a skill and process like rational discourse, a window to the world opens for us that otherwise is not in our vantage point about ourselves, another, or life itself.

As we emerge from chapter 1 and transition into chapter 2, simple questions and opportunities come to mind. What are the conditions outside yourself that allow you to look at yourself honestly and clearly? What do you think about your life? Are you clear about your mission, your legacy, your potential, and the impact you're having on others? Lying on your deathbed and looking back over your life, what would you feel was unfinished? Is your story authentic? Is it honest? Are you owning all your issues as you look at the world that you've created? Hopefully, you have a clear sense of who you are. That clarity will bring you to the doorstep of potential change.

CHAPTER 2

BEGINNING YOUR JOURNEY

Nothing really happens until change begins. And change doesn't happen until you are motivated and ready to begin the process. You've examined yourself and have begun to look at the gaps between who you are and who you might want to be; we called it the story of you. Most likely if you are reading this book, you are thinking about change, growth, and development, about getting on a new path. Likely, the *you* that you found does not match up with the *you* that you would like to be. That is a good start, but it is not enough to motivate and keep you on the path to realized change.

We'll now explore the process of change in adults. I'll argue that change is very much possible, but it requires the proper mix of ingredients to make it really happen. From my experience both professionally and personally, a small percentage of change goals that people have willfully and with all good intentions result in the successful matriculation of those changes. Why is that number so low? We would not tolerate such a pitiful rate of success in most any aspect of our lives, let alone the most important aspects of our lives—ourselves, our success, and our effectiveness.

There is an art and a science to change. The science involves discipline and focus, and the art requires passion, motivation, and a sense of urgency and importance. If you are to really take action, it will require that you develop confidence in your ability to change.

Confidence is fleeting. It ebbs and flows, and to keep it strong, we must continually feed it and cultivate it. We need to commit to it not just once but over time by initiating a set of practices, a discipline that will keep change in the forefront. We build confidence through our successes and by overcoming our failures. The important thing is to stay focused on the goal and the things that are done in small increments to bring you closer to that goal.

I have been working on a change in myself for the past few years. It is a big one in my life, and I am making progress by using some of the tools and ideas I will share with you in this chapter. I hope that sharing it with you will give you a better sense of how the process of changing or evolving oneself works and how you might apply the principles and tools on your own journey.

In my story, there is an element in my upbringing where I am trapped by my mom, literally and figuratively. She literally locked me in the house; two of her baby boys passed away at birth or shortly thereafter, and she did not want to lose me too. She developed an obsessive-compulsive neurosis and was in and out of mental hospitals during her life. In her obsession to control herself, she looped me into the program and made me obsessively check things with her to be sure all was OK. In my teen years, as I wanted to spread my wings, it became so difficult, and I wanted to rebel, but as it is with mental illness, I was trapped in its web.

The rage built inside me and, at times, would come out in fights with my mom, but I was ultimately submissive to her for many reasons. She was so damn powerful, and I wanted to respect and help her. I also felt sorry for her. In this situation, I lost my voice and my power. The anger and stored-up rebellion stewed inside me.

It seems to still be in my body now well into my seventies. When a situation develops with my wife, Teresa, or perhaps at work, and I feel controlled or mistreated, the anger comes out, and I am not my best self. I become loud and verbally aggressive, and I am mostly unable to listen.

The change I have been working on is to be more aware of these situations as they emerge in my life, to feel the emotions bubble up and pay attention to them. When I get into a situation like this now, I am able to recognize it and push the pause button, breathe, and count to ten. In that place, I can then gather myself and remember the values that I hold deeply in my life of respect and honoring the other and, of course, listening and finding the truth of the problem at hand. It's a bit like AA, I am sure, where each day, each week, I have to admit the challenge and work through the processes that help me to bring my best self forward.

There is surely a psychological component of this work, but there is also a science component. I am constantly practicing and learning about the micro-skills necessary to pull off this kind of change. An example would be the ability to slow the mind down enough to be able to feel and see what is happening in the moment. Another is the ability to listen empathically, to understand the other person and their feelings and to focus not only on myself. This is a process, no doubt, but one in which I have seen and felt progress. That progress gives me hope that I can overcome this dynamic of my life.

Perhaps you can think of a part of you that you would like to change or grow to be more effective, happier, or successful in your life. I noticed that the psychological remnants of my growing up were at the helm of my ship, so to speak. The part of me that was controlled by my mom now wanted to control others. Can you think of a part of you that is a remnant from your childhood or family dynamics that is dominating your beliefs or actions in your life? Is there a part of you that you would like to change? Realization is an opportunity for change; as it unfolds, you will be able to apply the tools and ideas we'll discuss in helping you to change yourself and your life.

The Process of Change

There are certain steps necessary to change a component of yourself, but before we look at these steps, there is one more thing to clarify. When I speak of changing yourself, it could be either of two things: adding a habit to increase your ability to change or removing a maladaptive behavior that is limiting your effectiveness. The former comes from vision, aspiring to be a better person. The latter comes from soul searching and looking at the story of *you*, seeing a gap or challenge that you wish to change. Either one of these strategies works, and the same principles will apply. When you glimpse a better way, creating an aspirational vision of yourself, and when you identify what is getting in your way, you will have found a motivation to change. You will have answered for yourself the question of what's in it for you. This is the energy needed to kickstart the process. It usually evolves from the gap between your aspiration and a true diagnosis of the current reality of your life. When the gap is significant, it opens the door for that motivation to enter. The trick is always timing; too early could equal not enough motivation, and too late could be debilitating and could create a sense of futility. Certainly, getting a bit ahead of the curve is helpful in change.

Wisdom begins with the definition of terms and knowledge about a field of study. If we want to change—say—how well we listen, then, in addition to assessing the gap, we would need to know what makes for great listening and how a high performer in this area does it.

The extent to which we know about ourselves is critical. Where is this behavior coming from, and what is it fulfilling in our quest to be safe and secure? Kegan talks about this as our immunity to change, which describes the pattern of behavior and beliefs that keeps us in the current loop of our behavior and sabotages our ability to change.

Your brain has an immense capacity to change and grow, but it will not do so easily. It needs you to signal a high level of interest, motivation, and clarity about what the change is and how it will improve your life. It also works best if you have a sense of urgency about the change—if you believe it is extremely important. This focus and urgency produce the physiological stimulants necessary to promote the brain to open up and learn new things.

Once you open that door and step through, it becomes important to set yourself up for success by having the right conditions and support around you. This might include a social support group, a loved one, a list, a chart, or simply a pat on the back.

This stage is more about discipline in the execution of the change, which involves patterns of success, like in training for a marathon. You need to have a plan and keep a chart of your activity to train your body and mind to do something outside of the normal pattern that it has worked into a groove over many years.

Recognizing success—whether it is small or large—is also critical. Most people who are successful in change and growth review progress at key milestones to celebrate and to look at how to improve the process, which is sometimes called an after-action review.

The final step is to loop back and remember the goal and motivation and to bring that success into the identification of the next change goal in your journey to becoming the person you hope to be. With that quick outline of the steps in the process of changing yourself, let's take a deeper dive into some of these areas to understand how we can best access them and achieve our goals for change.

The Anatomy of Behavior Change

If we are to change our behavior patterns, we need to understand how behavior forms, is nurtured, and sustains itself. As we begin this discussion, it would be useful for you to think of a behavior that is either an effective or less effective one that is an important part of your behavior pattern and your life. Understanding that behavior pattern in depth is like being an archeologist on a dig looking for artifacts that provide information about a civilization. Where do you look to find examples? What do they look like? Are they good or maladaptive behaviors? Do you understand how they are used and in what situation? Essentially, you are trying to uncover what belief—either good or not so good, true or not so true—is generating the thought pattern to drive this behavior.

Take a look at Figure 2.1. Let's start by looking above the water line, at the habits or behaviors someone would see in you or that you might be able to identify in yourself. Say you are fearful of confrontation or conflict with others. You can look below the surface of this habit and begin to ask questions about its root cause, where it comes from inside of you, and what its core dynamic is. If you go to the situational thoughts and feelings part of the triangle, you can observe that certain situations trigger useful or useless feelings or thoughts, which, in turn, drive that habit.

Origins of Our Habitual Behaviors

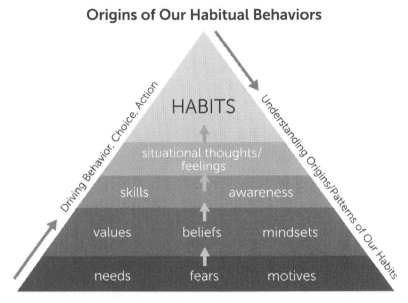

Figure 2.1

When I am faced with a potential conflict with another person, my thoughts usually are along these lines: This is going to be difficult and scary and someone is going to get their feelings hurt, or I will be forced to say things that I really do not care to share. I am likely to feel that I will be disliked because of sharing my thoughts. This tendency over time keeps getting reinforced, and the pattern solidifies. Hiding my true feelings becomes a habit, which has its origins deep inside me. What you would see without any transparency on my part would be me trying to make things OK, perhaps sublimating my needs or wants and feeling angry or frustrated internally, all of which will eventually cause a deterioration of the relationship and trust in each other. The impact is negative.

The next level down in the triangle is the awareness or skill level. Clearly, if I don't know any better, don't have a better model, I really have no path to success. If I am not even aware of the problem, how could I solve it? Without awareness, we don't really have a chance to change.

Think about the flip side: You do have a sense of right and wrong, and you can look at yourself and even ask for feedback. Imagine the positivity that would result if you could open up a conversation about your feelings and also about the situation at hand. It would be more effective if you had the skills to be able to describe your feelings. You would use *I* statements and own your side of the issue. You'd take responsibility for it. But to get there, you have to build your skills to be able to actually participate in that conversation effectively.

Your values, beliefs, and mindset occupy the next level in the anatomy of behavior triangle. Driving the habit is a faulty belief that full transparency and honesty will hurt feelings and ultimately put you in a dangerous situation. A misguided and maladaptive value set tells you to play it safe and not rock the boat. The most basic level of the faulty logic thread in this example is that of needs, fears, and motivation.

Each of us has a set of core issues that we most likely developed in our childhood and that has stayed with us and become a habit driving our behavior even as adults, professionals, leaders, and husbands. Although we occupy those mature personalities, we are operating from the fears of a five-year-old or possibly a young teen. These core fears are powerful and drive us to control situations, to protect ourselves at all costs, or to be overly compliant to safeguard our inner child. These fears seem real; they are in our body and drive habits over the course of our lives.

Our behavior and the resulting habits are not at all random; they are very purposeful and are aimed at keeping our persona intact. This is a very important function for a psyche that is less developed and less skillful. The habit is expertly crafted by the mind to keep us from dealing with the reality of the situation and the necessary resolution.

Our actions, words, and choices matter. They ultimately make up our personality, our character, and our legacy. Our life is the sum of our behaviors, and our behaviors are a function of our habits—conscious or not. If we are to truly change ourselves, we must be aware of this dynamic and seek to understand the elements below the water in the triangle to be able to change our behavior at the root, to change ourselves now and forever.

How Does Change Happen for Adults?

How adults change is an area of human development that I have studied extensively for the past thirty years, and there are some fascinating research, theories, and practices that I want to share with you. How change happens in adults is the holy grail of change research. Most everything else that is written about change in adults is about the context that adult humans need before they become interested in change and are then willing to try to change. Likely, the bottom line for all of us in becoming the person we hope to be, to achieve the greatness we seek, to discover and use our superpowers will require us to break down our goals and be about the change process.

Following is some of the most helpful and important research in this area that I have found. After laying it out, I will break it down for you into the most manageable chunks that I can so that you can apply these principles to your goals to change and work toward becoming the person you hope to be. There are three major pieces of the puzzle I would like to share with you toward that end:

· Research from the bestselling book *Change or Die* by Alan Deutschman

- · The six stages of experiential learning from Dr. David Kolbe
- · Kolbe's groundbreaking research on how adults learn

I will also be using work from Dr. Andrew Huberman, a professor of neuroscience in the medical school at Stanford University.

The first source that grabbed my attention was a book written by Alan Deutschman, who was a science writer for the *New York Times* and wrote a bestselling book called *Change or Die.* This is a catchy title for sure, and it conveys a sense of the importance of change. It also beckons the bottom line, which is that people are more likely to change when there is an extreme sense of urgency—even up to life-or-death stakes.

For many of us, our current life does bring us to that point. We feel life is so bad that we are at a tipping point. As bad as that sounds, it is good medicine for change. Better medicine would be to be able to decide to change and actually follow through when you are a bit ahead of the curve and not yet at a point of desperation. Thomas Watson, former CEO of IBM, said the best time to plan, set goals, and change is when you are on the crest of the wave, when things are going well. This reminds us that unless we are changing, we will die. It is the law of the living and the universe that decay and decline will happen without paying attention to what needs to change.

In his research about change, Deutschman drew from three important areas of research to write his book. Those areas were therapeutic communities working with psychological disorders or anxiety, individuals who had undergone a brain injury and were on the path to rehabilitation, and heart attack patients. What he found out is important to all of us as we think about our own quest for change.

First, from the psychological community, he found that working in a support group was one of the most critical aspects needed for change. He reminds us that humans are social beings and that we grow and change in communities of like-minded people. The concept of making our challenges and goals more transparent to others and involving the others in our process may be one of the most important things that we can do to help us to change. Decades of research with Alcoholics Anonymous has shown the power of a support group to both share issues and discover strategies to help us to change.

The second area is that of research from individuals who either had strokes or accidents that resulted in a lack of mobility; they were unable to walk or use other parts of their body. Deutschman found that one of the most important components of change is repetition. Forging or reforging neuropathways to signal the return of the new motor skill was critical. What this means for us is that, if we're going to change, we need to understand that an ongoing focus, daily repetition, and awareness of the change are critical. In many ways, as we change aspects of life, we will be forging new neural pathways and illuminating old habits.

The third area of his research was with heart attack patients. After a person has a heart attack, there seems to be great motivation to change their lifestyle, like eating habits and exercise and sleep. Deutschman found, however, that the newfound lifestyle was not long-lived; it waned over the next several months, and the person went right back to living life the way that they always had. He also found that there were some rehabilitation clinics that had had success over the long term with patients sustaining the changes. The difference was that in these programs the rehab was more holistic in nature and involved changes to the total lifestyle of the person. The motivation for change was drastically improved because it became a component of the day-to-day life of the person moving forward.

For our changes to stick, there needs to be important context and motivation for the change, and there needs to be a high level of engagement on the part of the individual who is changing to make it stick; that's you. These three strategies become extremely important for change to really happen but also for us to be able to sustain the change.

The Six Stages of Experiential Learning

There is a specific linear process that works best in adults to expand the brain and allow learning and change habits. David Kolbe performed his research at the graduate school at Case Western University. His work was the subject of my own doctoral dissertation in psychology at the University of Connecticut. Kolbe found that a six-step process worked best to initiate, explore, and anchor change in what he called *experiential learning.* Experiential learning is most likely a better approach overall in learning, but it is critical for adults. Let's learn about this process in hopes that you might apply it to your learning on your journey.

We can use an example from my own life of a problem that I often have in conversation with my wife, Teresa. When we have something to discuss, her style is to initially explore it openly and to keep it open and discover the best solution over time together. I seem to be more impulsive and tend to get roped in quickly and want to solve it very fast. When I do this, she feels uncomfortable, and it often leads to ill feelings for both of us. Here is how we might apply the model.

STEP 1: RECOGNITION

The first step is recognition. This is when we recognize that we have a gap or a problem. It doesn't matter if that comes to your attention because of feedback from someone else or whether you figure it out yourself. In this stage, your concern is to gain awareness of what behavior or habit you are exhibiting and when it is occurring. The challenge is more about identifying a problematic habit and registering the opportunity to change.

In this case, I have registered the gap of discomfort stemming from the differences in my approach and my wife's. My goal is to reserve judgment, to avoid rushing toward a solution, and to stay in a listening and open space. In this stage, it is critical that we also know what the good side of the behavior looks like, so we might need to go to step 2 to accomplish this.

STEP 2: UNDERSTANDING

Step 2, Understanding, is where we learn about the impact of what we are doing or trying to change and come to understand the way our behavior lands on the other person. We also understand why it is happening in us. It is also helpful to learn about the details and rationale of the positive side of fixing this habit.

In my example, I explore the problem with Teresa and find out how she experiences my behavior, which I may have only speculated about before speaking with her. I also strive to better understand what the behavior looks like when it is done well. I might read about it or listen to a YouTube video about it to raise my understanding.

STEP 3: ASSESSMENT

In this stage, you must see how your behavior matches up with the ideal behavior identified in step 2. When I do this, I am trying to calibrate how much of a problem this is for me and the other person, and I am assessing the impact as well. I sometimes put a number on it, from 1 being very poor at this skill to 5 being world class. In my case, I am a 2, but I am hoping over the next several months to become a 4. I could continue to ask Teresa and others for feedback about how I am doing, and I can ask myself and her what behaviors I could start, stop, or continue that would move me from a 2 or 3 to a 4 in this makeshift assessment scale. Measurement is key because it helps to concretize and quantify the behavior.

STEP 4: EXPERIMENTATION

This stage is critical to experiential learning. As you try out your new behaviors in the world, you learn how to do them better. Experimentation is a way to understand what is good and bad in the moment. It is sometimes hard to improve a skill based only on reading or talking about it; doing it and then looking at your performance and getting feedback are much more helpful.

In my example, I pay attention to my reactions in not-so-hard situations just to learn more about them. What I find is that I am not really being open and still driving too hard for solutions; I have difficulty staying in the moment and not projecting the outcomes I fear. By experimenting with different responses in low-stakes interactions, I can hone my skills for the higher stakes.

STEP 5: PRACTICE

In this step, the objective is to practice the new behavior or skill in real-time situations. Sometimes, it's helpful to prep for the upcoming experience and map out how you might approach it—what you might say, what you might do, and what you want to feel. This preparation is really helpful to keep you on track. Once again, after the practice, you can get feedback from the other person and course correct on your approach.

In my example, Teresa and I anticipated a situation coming up, and I had a chance to do some thinking and planning to practice the new behavior in the way that I had mapped out in an earlier stage. Doing this preparation really helped me to stay in the moment and to focus on the skills that I was learning and wanted to practice.

STEP 6: APPLICATION

During the application stage, after going through experimentation and practice, you can begin to apply the new behavior in real situations. Hopefully, you will find that all of your thinking and preparation have really paid off and that you have really started to integrate the new behavior into the fabric of your life and relationships.

In my situation, I have a much greater awareness when I notice the feeling inside and stop and think—perhaps count to ten—and move into the new behavior pattern that I had practiced. If you think about getting better at a sport or improving something at work, you most likely use this approach unconsciously, and it surely is the way to increase your performance in those areas of your life as well.

I have found the experiential learning model extremely helpful to step through the actions and mental preparation that I need to be able to integrate a new habit into my life.

Changing your life is essentially about breaking the habits that you have invested in creating to live your life successfully. Once you have the motivation to try new things, using this approach will be extremely helpful.

Neuroscience and Brain Plasticity Research

The third and final piece of the puzzle of changing yourself is neuroplasticity, the ability for your brain to rewire itself. The science of the brain has made massive leaps in the past five years, and we are discovering the vast power of the brain to change and grow even as you read. As I was researching this area for the book and for my own edification in my personal change process, this area emerged as the most useful and exciting.

The story starts with the notion that the human brain is fully developed by age twenty-five. That only means that the circuitry is complete and the connections established and well honed. It does not mean that additional capacity cannot be added or current circuits changed and enhanced.

Here is how it works, in a nutshell. Our IQ peaks in our late thirties, but our brain remains plastic—changeable. The key to plasticity is motivation, the sense of urgency, and the focus and discipline to change a habit.

When we discussed the anatomy of behavior, we learned that maladaptive habits or behaviors have their origins deeper in the human psyche and that they evolve into the belief systems and decisions that we make. Those patterns of behavior are highly grooved into our neuropathways to produce regular unconscious actions—habits. When we want to change our behavior, we either want to eliminate a maladaptive behavior or introduce a new behavior or skill into our patterns.

Brain research indicates that a particular set of conditions must be present for the brain to change at a later stage in life. I'd like to describe this to you in terms of the motivation that would be necessary to be able to initiate and sustain the change. In order to get the brain to produce the proper mix of physiological chemicals like dopamine and acetylcholine which actually produce a change in the brain's chemistry, there needs to be a sense of urgency that gets us excited enough to be able to come to the doorstep of change.

This is similar to the fight-or-flight response of a caveman during prehistoric times. When our caveman friend saw a saber-toothed tiger, chemicals were produced in his brain that allowed him to bring forth his maximum strength for the battle. If your brain perceives a sense of urgency for change—in this case, based on the amount of pain that you are experiencing in your life—the opportunity for change presents itself to the brain.

You might ask yourself what would create that sense of urgency or motivation to change. This is a critical question, and only you will be able to answer it. Clearly, it needs to be extremely important to you. Change is hard, and to follow through with it, you must see a better and healthier life, a more fulfilling life as the prize at the end of the journey. This is your first job: See that well-lived life.

Your second job in changing yourself is creating focus. Once you have the attention of your brain, you have the possibility of changing it. But you need to direct the change, and direction comes from the micro-identification of the goals or behaviors that you want to bring into your life. Focus is created when we navigate the fine line between understanding what needs to change and selecting the specific behaviors that need to be developed. When we combine focus with a sense of urgency and do so over time, the brain has the possibility of changing.

The third crucial element is discipline. You need discipline to stay focused and continue that sense of urgency, that continued activity that will sustain the change over time. It is much like trying to build muscle: You can improve for a while, but if you don't continue to exercise the specific muscle, it will atrophy. The same is true in your brain. The change that you are seeking will need that same continued focus and energy.

One of the other critical components for creating new connections in your brain—from maladaptive to positive behavior patterns—is your brain's need for rest. It turns out that the actual change occurs during deep sleep. In a sense, what you're doing is setting the change up during your waking hours so that it completes the cycle during your sleep. The repetition of this process over time will result in new neural pathways in your brain that allow you to make better decisions and produce the habits and behaviors that you are seeking.

I have been experimenting with this process over the past year, trying to change some of my original behaviors. I've also tried it in accomplishing new goals in my life. I have been amazed at the spaciousness, openness, and creativity that I find my brain operating at, even at this stage of my life. If I had to put a number on it, I would say I've noticed a 25–35 percent increased capacity for learning, creativity, and change during this experimentation.

There are a multitude of ideas, tools, and practices available to you for changing yourself. Understanding them is critical and aiming them at the proper goal is equally critical. Your job is to bring yourself to the doorstep of change and growth. This motivation can only come from you; although others can help, it cannot be generated from outside of you. It is a decision you must make and live through.

I am in this process right now and have been for several years. During the past year of writing this book, I have noticed immeasurable change. As encouraging as that change is, I know that I will need to stay focused and stay in the growth and learning process on an ongoing basis to capitalize on these changes. I have seen that if I take my foot off the pedal of change in my life, I become complacent and I slip back into old habits.

Your self-diagnosis of needed change comes from your view of the outside world, as we discussed earlier. That view must be an accurate viewpoint to be a real catalyst for change. In a sense, that is an outside-in process. The redesign of your life is the opposite; it is an inside-out process, where you look inside to understand the root cause of your outer behavior patterns. You change the inside—the cause—first, and that internal change relieves the symptom. The inside changes will move up the triangle of behavior and start producing behaviors and habits that are more in alignment with your aspirational self, your personal vision of a well-lived life. This is a bit counterintuitive in that we typically look at behavior and outcomes from the outside and seek to change or alter the outer behaviors—usually with superficial change—and do not really address the inner conditions that are the origination of the problem.

CHAPTER 3

YOUR INNER SELF

Renowned psychologist Carl Jung observed the universal paradox of the inner self. For him, the inner self is inextricably formed by the inner child, by your experience growing up. This time was a powerful source of love, divinity, regeneration, and possible new beginnings. At the same time, it as a source of maladaptive behaviors, contamination, and destruction. The concept of the wounded inner child has become, in the past fifty years, a modern archetype, representing the vast potential of all humans and our unique and collective psychic inheritance. George Bernard Shaw described this view of the inner self, the inner child, when he wrote, "What is a child? An experiment. A fresh attempt to produce the just man . . . That is to make humanity divine." The concept of the inner self is a powerful driver of human behavior. It is an idea not to be toyed with but taken extremely seriously.

Let's begin with a quick recap of where our potential hero has been on this journey of a man so far. First, we explored the story of you, the outer life that you have crafted and honed for better or worse. Based on your level of awareness, self-reflection, and honesty, you have decided this persona is not the be-all and end-all for you and that there is a better you inside ready to be cultivated. That brought us to several important questions: Once you identify a gap or glimpse a better version of yourself, can you change and grow? How do you change? What would it take? This discussion helped us see that change is possible and even in the very mandate of what it means to be human—to adapt, evolve, and continue to better our families and species. The conclusion I hope that you gleaned from the discussion is that, yes, it is possible and exciting and gives great hope for each of us. But alas, it is not easy. It requires what all worthwhile things in life require: the time, attention, courage, and discipline needed to actually change. Bestselling author Malcolm Gladwell postulated in his book *Outliers* that it takes ten thousand hours to fine-tune any skill that would allow you to become world class at the skill. My bet is that very few of us have come close to that investment in ourselves and our development as adults, humans, and men.

The next stage, your inner self, is the origin of your behaviors. In order to begin your journey, you'll need to uncover your inner self, your private self. You may already be aware of some of it, but much of it may be surprising. You must also discover your aspirational inner self, the superpowers that you have, the values that, in the best version of yourself—which you have every right to—exist within you. Finally, you must recover your inner self, turn it into an integrated, aware, and conscious version of you through the resolution of all parts of you into a wholly mature, loving, and fully functioning man.

The great paradox of this section of the journey is that it is the most avoided part, the least examined, the hardest to deeply explore—but it is, by far, for the brave of heart, the most powerful and consequential element in your journey to a life well lived. It has been the hardest for me to look at in myself and along my journey, and it is the most difficult to write about. You have shown enough interest or curiosity to pursue the journey to this point. You are reading about it and hopefully will capture the power of change.

Some of the terrain that we will travel includes finding answers to the following questions:

- What are the inner self, the inner game, and your private self?
- How did your inner self come to be? What is your unique version of your story?
- What drives this aspect of yourself even to this day?
- How can you alter this powerful element that is driving your life?
- Can you sustain that change, and what is the ongoing work to embed this into your newly integrated self?

Here is how we're going to do this. First, I'm going to answer these five questions for you and just kind of get the basics out of the way. Then I'm going to tell you a story, sort of a case study of how my inner self has been alive and well in my life, driving in a great deal of my behavior, both positive and negative. Then I'm going to talk with you about the three stages of approaching the inner life.

Our first step in this process is learning about your inner self and uncovering the core issues in your life. These core issues are a combination of your DNA, your family dynamic, and your unique experiences.

Step 2 is to discover your inner self guidance system: This is where you think about and render the aspiration you have in your life that is important to you—for example, the vision of your life, your new values, your key motivations. The things that drive you in your life when you have the chance to think deeply about your life purpose.

Step 3, recovering your inner self, is about integrating the inner you that you discovered in uncovering yourself, integrating it with the discovered person that you thought about in step 2, and coming up with a third version that is more resolved. We may find that, perhaps, a blend of masculine and feminine energies and a way for you to operate in your life effectively will move you closer to your aspirational self.

What Is the Inner Self?

Your inner self can be more or less conscious in your life. You might be very aware of some of the feelings and core issues that seemed to be important to you—either positive or negative—and that drive a number of your behaviors. One way to help you understand the power of the inner self is to think about a very simple framework that I learned about in an introductory psychology course in college. It's called the see–do–get model.

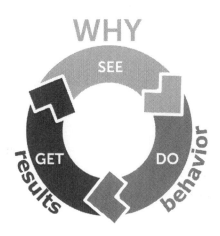

Figure 3.1

As you can see from Figure 3.1, our behaviors begin in the twelve o'clock position with seeing. The critical piece of any situation is to ask where your unhealthy behaviors come from. They certainly don't come out of nowhere; they must be generated from you, your brain, your thought patterns, or your motives. That is where the *see* portion of the model comes into play. Seeing is the genesis of our behaviors and our results. How we see the world—our paradigms of how things work—drives our behavior and our actions. For example, if we see the world as a dangerous place, cutthroat, and every man for himself, then you can imagine the impact on your view of the world, on your behaviors, and ultimately on the results. Imagine you are a leader of a big organization and you have this view of the world; you would be tremendously competitive and aggressive in your decision-making. You could also imagine that that behavior could drive incredible short-term performance but might lead to problems in the long run.

We then move to the two o'clock position, with doing. *C* stands for the behaviors, actions, or decisions that you make in your life at any time. They could be big decisions or little decisions, small actions or complex actions.

Doing leads directly to *getting.* Whatever you do has a lot to do with what you get in your life, so there's a very strong relationship between the *do* arrow and the *get* arrow. In this model, *get* stands for the results that you get in your life. They are the outcomes produced by the behaviors you perform.

The key question in using this model is: If you want to get better results, where should you focus your energy? The obvious answer is to focus on your behaviors because they have the strongest connection to your results. But the more accurate answer is that the way you see the world is based on your core beliefs. Your inner self drives the processes, thought patterns, and paradigms that determine your behavior and, ultimately, your results. If you wanted to make an incremental change in your results, then you might change a behavior and deal only with the symptoms of the problem. If you wanted to create substantial, long-term results, then you would change how you see the world, your core paradigms, your core beliefs. Those beliefs drive your behaviors and the results you're getting. With that understanding of the importance of our core beliefs and inner self, let's continue our exploration.

Consider the notion of the inner self, where it comes from, how it came to be, and how it operates in your life. If you look at the see–do–get model, you can see that the *see* portion is the composite of your beliefs. Your view of the world has been cultivated carefully via your key experiences, role models, family dynamics, work experiences, perhaps even your ethnic heritage, and certainly whether you are a man or a woman. One thing is for sure: Your inner self is yours—uniquely yours. It is in your DNA, and it is very alive and well and has a big job to do in your life: to keep your self-image intact and to keep you safe. The inner self—bad or good—likely has its hands on the steering wheel of your life as you are driving down the road at 80 mph. Whether you are conscious of it or not, it is a powerful dynamo that drives your behavior.

INNER VERSUS OUTER SELVES

The inner self filters every thought, decision, and action you make, but it is often hidden from view—from you and others. If you could unlock it and expose it, many things would become clear and make more sense, and that is exactly what we are going to do.

In contrast with the outer self, the inner self is what can't be seen: feelings, intuition, values, beliefs, personality, thoughts, emotions, fantasies, desires, and purpose. If you have a strong inner self, it means that you deal well with your emotions, are aware of your own feelings, hold clarity and a good sense of your values, and see your purpose in life. In addition, you are likely able to remain centered and calm in the face of challenges and downturns in life from the outer world. With a well-developed sense of self—a mature self—the inner and outer selves are in harmony.

Problems tend to come up when the inner self and the outer self are in disagreement or when there is a gap between what the inner self thinks is right and what the outer self does out of reactivity. When our inner life is not cultivated, it's like we are running on empty and become more vulnerable to illness and difficulty in relationships. We feel that we are not aligned with our values and that dissonance creates stress and tension. If you have experienced this, it likely stuck with you. It's hard to think of anything else when your inner life is out of balance.

Hopefully, it is clear that your inner life is a strong component of your life, but you may not have a great deal of self-awareness of how this unconscious motivation engine is making decisions for you. When the shadow side of our inner life is not known or not owned, we have a tendency, unconscious though it may be, to project those undesirable aspects of the self onto other people. A healthy resolution of this is individuation, which includes developing an awareness of your projections and withdrawing them.

We may not actually alter the shadow inner self a great deal, although that is possible, but we can mitigate its effects in our life through awareness and through our choices of behavior. Self-awareness, therefore, becomes the key to success in this area. Through self-awareness, we see ourselves more accurately, and this can be the starting point of change.

THE ORIGIN OF YOUR INNER SELF

For most men, there is thought to be an existential and universal moment in time, usually around five years old, when we start to become disconnected from ourselves. In general, the situation goes like this: The boy has feelings or fears and begins to express them to his parents or other adults. Those adults downplay and even refute those feelings, and the boy realizes that having feelings and fears is not a good thing, or at least not something he is supposed to share. He makes a decision to hold them in to gain greater harmony with what others seem to value, and at that time, the journey toward disconnecting with the inner self begins; it is then reinforced in many ways over time.

Let me share an example of this from my childhood. I call it "Wherever I go, there I am!" As you read it, take note of the inner self that emerges and what elements in my situation growing up fueled this core issue and belief system that has driven me in my life. You might think of a similar story or set of events in your life. What do you think your core inner self issue is?

A difficult childhood and family situation were my lot in life from the earliest age that I can recall, and they continued for most of my life, through and into my forties and fifties; remnants certainly still exist today. I will describe the dynamics of my family of origin in detail in a later chapter, but for now, my mother, Mary, was severely challenged by her family dynamic. Her parents, Joseph and Antionette DelBouno, arrived from southern Italy via Ellis Island in the 1920s searching for the American dream. They had six children of which my mom was the second oldest. The family was poor, and both of my grandparents worked long shifts in manufacturing companies, leaving little time for attending to the family. Money was scarce and my grandmother—we called her Mama—forced my mom to drop out of high school to take care of the family. My mother excelled academically and had dreams of being a professional person. The family—or at least my experience of it as a young person—was very dysfunctional and placed a heavy weight of uncertainty, fear, and insecurity on my mom. The trauma of her childhood and how she was treated hurt her to the core, and that core wound—or wounds—waited just below the surface but inevitably came rushing out as her life become complicated in her mid-thirties. The core wounds and trauma were multiplied exponentially when she had two baby boys who died at birth or soon thereafter. She became mentally unstable, aggressive, and dominating, and was clinically diagnosed as an obsessive–compulsive neurotic. She was in and out of mental institutions for much of my early years and received electric shock treatments. Because she was quite intelligent (she was valedictorian of every school she attended), and she was quite persuasive, she figured out how to talk her way out of the mental institution. Once she was out, she refused treatment and wreaked havoc on the lives of everyone around her—my sister, Dolores; my dad, Big Tony; myself; and all our relatives. She was out of control in her life, and she aimed her instability at our family. I was particularly at risk as I was the only boy child, and although she revered me, she was terrified of losing me, resulting in the origins of my core dynamic or challenge that has followed me and even controlled me, as it did for Mother Mary her entire life.

We all have our stories and responses to those stories, and my evolution while getting through that hell of a childhood may have created coping and adaptive mechanisms that propelled me to high achievement in many aspects of life. But that same experience also left a big psychological mark on me, inside and outside. I was blessed with the resilience to keep my sense of self. I became a fierce warrior for myself, with the enemy being Mary and anything the opposite of her way of living. It was tremendous motivation, but I never attended to the inner scars of that child, teenager, or young adult. Inside, I was angry, fragile, uncertain, with little or no voice or proper frame on the world.

Outside, I was a bedwetter until my mid-teens. I was shy and an underachiever. I managed to build my strength and my self-image as time went on, but it was a house of cards. I was a high achiever in the later stages of college, a Division 1 multisport athlete. I excelled in most areas of my life. I was so motivated to understand myself and to not be like Mary or her family. I vowed to study psychology at the highest level to be sure that I wouldn't go crazy like my mom told me her psychiatrist said I would. I was able to attain a master's degree in counseling psychology and a doctorate in psychology by age thirty. My careers flourished and life unfolded on the exterior, but the inside game was never at peace, and I found that, indeed, wherever I went, there I was.

The warrior inside me had a mature and positive side and also a shadow and maladaptive side, both of which are still alive in me and motivate my behavior. You might imagine the power that motive had to propel me to work hard, succeed, and excel at many things in an effort to cover up my inside wounds. On the other side, this aggressiveness and controlling behaviors propelled me to be highly competitive and willing to do a great deal to avoid losing at the highest level. Interpersonally, in my relationships with others close to me, that behavior pattern can be challenging and even gets me in arguments with my wife; I am so hell-bent on getting my way or being in charge.

With continued effort toward many of the techniques in this book, I have softened and become a better partner, husband, father, leader, and friend. What is clear to me in all this is the point of this chapter: The inner self, our core issues and dynamic, is a strong determinant or our behavior. Change will not likely happen without addressing this part of ourselves.

I describe this inner self as your core operating system, your OS. It is much like the OS that drives a computer system in that its logic— either faulty or sound—is the very thing that drives all its functions. Trying to fix the computer or an application without understanding the inherent OS just does not work. The same is true for you in your life: Trying to work on only the outside will likely not work. It needs to be an inside job.

Three Steps of the Inner Life Journey

Let's shift our attention to the three steps in the inner life journey that I described earlier: uncover, discover, and recover. I will describe each and give you a process to move through the steps to achieve a positive resolution for you in your hope to better understand your inner self and the origin of your behavior and habits.

STEP 1: UNCOVER

If it is true that the inner self guides much of your behavior in the outer world, then uncovering your OS is important. How can you do that without years of therapy? Let me break it down for you. The following process and questions are a sort of workshop you can take yourself through initially and then repeat, perhaps monthly, as you gain more knowledge and understanding of yourself.

The notion of uncovering is based on the premise that inside your psyche and mind and heart there are voices that are less conscious or even unconscious that guide your every thought and action. As we saw in my story, and if we look at what Robert Kegan's stages of adult development offer us, our persona, or outer self, is dedicated to the proposition that we can craft an outer self that can remain safe and intact even in the face of a seemingly dangerous world. Major research studies have shown that 65 percent of men are in the socialized-self stage of adult development. This stage is a reactive rather than pro-active stage, in that we craft our habits and mindset in response to a set of fears inside of us that may or may not be accurate versions of the real world. The hard part is that we mostly don't know whether the view is accurate or not. We honestly believe something is off or threatening, and that may be purely in our heads.

In addition, the last thing that a man wants to do is share his inner feelings! For men, most of life is directly in front of them. We are highly focused, very task oriented, and not likely to consider anything else unless there is a serious problem. That is often exactly what is needed to wake us up to what is really happening in front of us and then what is behind the curtain. In a real sense, that is how much of our lives are lived. When things are going along fine and then a wake-up call happens, we are forced to address the issues that have been at the center of our behavior—the inner life—the entire time.

As I write, I am dealing with an issue like this today. I have been feeling a bit depressed and overly reactive to a number of things. That often oozes out in my relationship with Teresa. When she brought up that the usual sparkle in my eye had not been there for some time, I knew that she was correct. I was struggling in my inner life, where I often hide until I am called out. You might be able to relate.

I am very motivated to change and am going to address this as soon as I am able. I would bet you might be interested in what I am going to do about it. I thought you would never ask!

For starters, just becoming aware of the behaviors and the impact on my loved one is a strong start to motivating me to look at this behavior and work on it. I would need to go deeper to understand the feelings and then the outer behaviors that are coming up and out. I am in that process now. Some additional things that I have done in the past that help are as follows:

- Remember and focus on the love and admiration I have for my wife and our relationship over the years. Focus on what a loving and wonderful person she is in every way.

- Focus on my values, what is important to me, and how I can be more aligned with those values at this time.

- Invest more time in our relationship and time together, the things we love to do.

- Deepen my meditation and journaling process to get in touch with my inner self.

- Develop a greater awareness of my feelings and behaviors in real time and stop myself from overreacting.

Here is what you can do to uncover the inner you:

- Get in touch with the feelings you are experiencing and get more conscious about naming them and owning them.

- Feel the tension in your body when it comes up for you.

- Notice the things that are challenging for you to do in your life; they are indications of areas that are cause for concern inside you.

- Notice the challenges that others are having with you. Ask for feedback and explore this in a deeper manner.

- When you feel irritable and unloving, see if you can trace the feelings and behaviors into your body and then to a more central core issue or gap in your life.

Overall, ask yourself what the patterns are that you see inside and outside yourself. See if you can identify the core drivers of those elements. There are three core issues from the research that seem to drive us in our shadow and reactive life:

- The desire to control situations and interactions so that you can remain safe;

- Protecting yourself from others or difficult situations; and

- Compliance, where we defer our own self-interest to another in an attempt to be liked or get approval.

In general, a large portion of our brain's real estate is mostly taken up by elements that inform us to fight or flee from danger. We are wired to protect ourselves with one or more of those strategies. This comes to us legitimately, as millions of years of DNA refinement has led us to that place.

Our inner life OS is heavily oriented toward keeping us safe. What we are uncovering are the maladaptive strategies that have been created in our lives to keep us safe and to keep our self-concept intact.

STEP 2: DISCOVER

Once we have a better sense of our personal OS, we can begin to understand it better in hopes of creating healing or mitigation approaches, like counting to ten. The discovery stage of dealing with the inner life is a bit more creative, forward thinking, and deeply important to us. We are more used to using this part of our brains as we think deeply about our lives, our goals, and what is important to us.

One way to think about this is to imagine it is your eightieth birthday party and all the important folks in your life are present: your family, friends, colleagues, and so on. Imagine that each person gets up one by one to pay tribute to you and your life. What would they say that would make you proud? What would be a worthy legacy of your life? What was the north star that led you in your life? What values drove you, and what was your mission in life? What are the chances that what folks would say about you is what you would like to be known for in your life? Then think about what you would like them to be saying. What are your aspirations? How well are you living that life?

This exercise is a great example of the discovery phase of the inner life journey. In a sense, you discover for yourself what is important in your life. How do you relate to others, and how consistent were you in living this way? You most likely already know what is important to you, although that might have changed if you haven't looked at yourself in this way in a while.

Figure 3.2

The discover phase is a critical piece of the process of change. Think of it this way: When you get a good sense of your current reality in the uncover stage, an honest and motivating assessment, and, at the same time, you hold a vision from the discovery phase as in the previous exercise, you create a natural tension in your life and consciousness. See Figure 3.2 as an example of that process.

Is the tension a good thing or a bad thing, and how might it be resolved? It is a bad thing if you let the gap fester and do nothing about it. That tension in your body and mind creates stress and tends to bring about illness and dismay. You might also see that tension as a motivator or accelerator to change. You can move toward the vision by setting goals and taking action, and you can also move away from your not-so-positive current behaviors, so that you move toward your vision of a life well lived. Using your discovery vision to propel your action toward that vision is a powerful resolution of the structural tension created in this process. Discovering your inner-self drivers and true values is the key to this process.

STEP 3: RECOVER

The process of resolving steps 1 and 2 into a version of your inner self that is integrated and fully conscious of the pieces operating in your life, inside and outside, is what the recover step is about. You might think about it as recovering from the you that is not fulfilling your aspirations of a better life.

Part of recovering is learning to covet yourself, to honor and deeply appreciate your gifts. You have to learn to be grateful for the positive things in your life. It is the opposite of covering up, as we often do in our outer life. That opposite would entail looking inside at the root cause of the pain or stress or disarray and addressing it with clarity, focus, compassion for yourself, patience, and discipline. This is the opposite of the disintegration of your inner self that happens without the level of consciousness that we have noticed about ourselves in our day-to-day trance state. Integration is bringing together the parts of your true self and dealing with them in a thoughtful manner.

I am recovering my true self when I acknowledge my feelings, when I am aware of my values, when I choose a more conscious path, when I work on myself and build my capability to be aware and choose to take actions that will move me toward my true self.

There are several steps you can take to fully recover your true self:

- Bring awareness to moment-to-moment situations, feelings, and interactions by checking in with yourself. Notice what you are feeling, thinking, and hoping. I call this awareness intelligence (AQ).

- When you do notice, you bring your full vision of your true inner self to the table to insert actions and behaviors that are more in keeping with your discovery from step 2 of the inner self journey. I call this choice intelligence (CQ). It tells us that there is a bigger *yes* burning inside that comes from our inner knowledge and values and that makes us able to say no to the feelings and negative tendencies that generally steer our lives.

- In order to have the presence of mind to be able to accomplish steps 1 and 2, you will need thoughtful and planned investment of yourself in cultivating a peaceful mind through the tools that we will suggest in a later chapter, such as meditation, breathing, exercise, non-sleep deep rest, and more. A quiet mind will allow you to do steps 1 and 2.

The experience of moving through the three steps outlined in this chapter will support you in getting in touch with your inner self. The inner self is the primary driver of our habits and our behaviors and is easily overlooked or misunderstood. We need to cultivate it to ensure it is in tip-top shape to bring your best self forward in life.

CHAPTER 4

VOICES OF THE REACTIVE MINDSET

A s a child, I greatly anticipated the yearly showing of *The Wizard of Oz*. You might bring back the feeling and experience of that time preparing yourself and your family for that magical night. Perhaps a bowl of popcorn, a warm blanket to hide behind for those scary scenes, and the greatly anticipated songs and marches that we all came to know and love. "We're off to see the Wizard, the wonderful Wizard of Oz!"

With many meaningful themes of life developed in the plot, Dorothy encounters the Tin Man, the Scarecrow, and the Lion, who become her support team in her adventure through the Land of Oz. They represent three important elements or voices of our self: the brain, the heart, and courage. They each seek that less developed part of themselves to make them whole. Ultimately, the Wizard and Dorothy award them these honors, bestowing upon them the disavowed part of themselves that they were seeking.

In a similar manner, you have voices inside you that represent aspects of yourself that are either underdeveloped or overly developed. Our hope in this chapter is to help you come to know them in yourself in an effort to build strength around them and mitigate their impact on your life and shift to voices that are more proactive, creative, empathic, and loving.

The infamous Wizard was mysterious and magical behind the curtain, and although he seemed otherworldly, in the end, he was a man trying to find his way on his journey. This chapter is a bit like that, but the wizard is you, and the elements of yourself are, in a sense, behind a curtain—some known by you and some not but surely pulling the levers that play a critical role in your life every day, hour, minute, and moment.

In the *G.I. Joe* series that was so popular back in the 1980s on TV and in comic books, a different hero ended each episode with a lesson about life, but their message was the same. "Now you know," the hero would say, "and knowing is half the battle." The message is that knowing is not the same as doing! Knowing from chapter 3 that we have an inner self that is powerful is indeed not enough; we need to do something about it to advance our journey toward a life well lived. We most likely want deep inside to be a superhero, like G.I. Joe, a Marvel character, or perhaps even the all-powerful Wizard of Oz.

In this chapter, we will dig deeper into all of this and begin to turn the corner to bring forth tools and processes that will shift your thinking and action from the reactive to the proactive mindset and bring out the superpowers in yourself and hopefully others in your life. Let's begin that leg of the journey now.

Let us assume the best—that each of us truly desires in the deepest part of ourselves to be a loving, caring, honest, trustworthy, and vital person in our lives and our relationships. No one likely gets up in the morning thinking, *I want to be a bad person today and hurt people's feelings. I want to be a part of a crappy work team or family.* We often collect ourselves in the morning to bring our best selves into our day. Yet these best-laid plans don't often materialize as our day starts to happen to us. Little by little, these challenges eat away at our clean slate, and we are no longer coming to them from a place of love and caring as we had hoped. It is like our resilience has been significantly diminished, and we find ourselves used up and stripped down to a part of ourselves that is raw and not as resourced. When this happens, we are more susceptible to the little or not-so-little things in front of us causing a totally inappropriate response. That response is likely to come from a place inside that is trying to do the right thing. Perhaps more importantly, it is trying to keep your ego intact above all else. *How could I possibly be the problem here? If only—why doesn't she see?* and *I cannot believe that!* are some responses we have in our internal dialogue in these situations.

I'll put myself on the couch for a minute here to give an example. I tend to sleep well, which helps in all of this. When I wake up in the morning, I am fresh, with a clean slate, and rested, ready to be my very best and live my mission and values. To add to that positivity, I am a morning person in my cycles of aliveness and creativity like many of you are as well. I might even plan my day and affirm my intentions. Likely, I would meditate, pray, and journal while listening to calming background music. I usually get up very early, around 5:30 a.m., to be sure that I have several hours to remember who and what I am striving for in my life. I have been doing this religiously for over thirty years. I am sure it has helped me tremendously to be more centered and loving in my day, and I am thankful for that. However, it is not the only reason I do it; I truly find peace and happiness in these practices each day.

71

In so doing, I am hoping to quiet the voices inside myself that seem to be ready to hijack my best plans from that morning retreat. I know that they are there, ready to rear their not-so-pleasant heads and take over from the peaceful and resilient voices that are with me in the morning. When I do this, I am trying to bring to the forefront my proactive, loving, and caring self and to mitigate or put in the background my reactive, stressful, angry, accusing self. If you are like me and many other men, this is a constant battle each day, each hour, each moment.

Unfortunately, at times—and surely during the 2020–21 pandemic—Teresa is the person with whom I have my first point of interaction in the morning. She is an incredibly loving, kind, thoughtful, creative, caring, and positive soul. She has been a delight to love and live with for the past thirty years. We often work together, have raised kids together, manage our home and lives together, and we often do things we love to do together, like hiking and biking and traveling—in the old days before the pandemic. My life generally is very blessed now; my health is stabilized since the cancer; my career is fun and successful; our extended family and friends are lovely and close to us, and we live in a beautiful home in a lovely part of the world.

The voices are, however, deep inside me. They are powerful forces that intercept my good intentions at times. A recent situation looked like this: Teresa and I were having our morning tea together and planning for the day. The subject of me seeing my doctor came up. I have a condition called CLL, chronic lymphoma cancer, that is low lying and can have effects on my immune system. It is reasonable for her to ask about it since she does care a great deal about me. At this point, a voice intercedes from my inner self. This voice evolved from my childhood and represents a strong part of my inner core and inner armor that learned to be fierce in taking care of myself and not relying on others. I feel anger come over me and frustration with my illness being brought up or Teresa even suggesting that I do something. Without taking hold of myself and my feelings, I become angry and raise my voice. I become argumentative with Teresa, wanting her to, in a sense, stay out of my boat or leave it to me to figure it out on my own. Probably like most men, I do have a tendency to let health issues go too long. But even so, I do not give her the grace for what she is asking me about and instead become upset and reactive. Of course, this begins to spiral and becomes a more difficult discussion, and we both get frustrated and feel disconnected. As I settle down after a while, I can see the part of me that overreacted to a simple question, and I feel sorry about how I handled the situation.

This example is typical for me in my relationship with Teresa, and I fight with myself a great deal to address it. The voices of the reactive mind take control of an interaction and hijack my good intentions. As if this were not bad enough, the escalation causes Teresa to find it difficult to share or bring things up with me. I would not like that to be the case, and we are working on this issue in our marriage as I write this. Some days I am better than on others. We will discuss that a bit later in this chapter and will also discuss how to begin to change this dynamic in yourself and with others.

Recall that we discussed two important theoretical constructs that I suggested were important in understanding the story of you. The first was the adult stages of development by Robert Kegan. We found that adults go through stages of human development and that most adults (58 percent) were in the socialized self stage of development, Kegan's stage 3. The hallmarks of stage 3 are that the individual is making decisions in life based upon ego and keeping the ego intact. In this phase, we are socializing our thinking so that we make decisions and react based upon this version of our persona that has been crafted over the years. The persona is very much reactive to the environment. The voices of the reactive mindset, being part of our core personas, become very powerful. They are the lead characters in the movie of our life. In a sense, they write the script for how we will think and speak in that movie.

Stages of Adult Development

by Dr. Robert Kegan

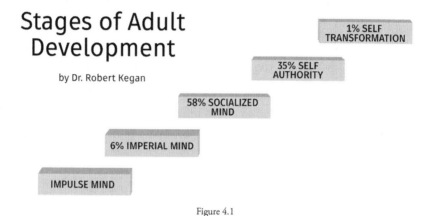

Figure 4.1

This as opposed to stage 4 of Kegan's model, which is the self-authoring stage. In this stage, adults make decisions and relate based on their values and internal choices rather than in relation to what others think. This is a more mature, advanced approach to life, as it breaks us free from the bonds of what other people think. It frees us from making decisions based on fear or some other reactive tendency. This is movement in general away from the voices of the reactive mindset and toward a voice that is resolved of one's inner critic and reactive tendencies. This operating system is designed more to go toward what is desired rather than to move away from fear. Research indicates that around 25 percent of the adult population in large samples across cultures are operating in this stage of human development.

When I found out about this research, I became consumed with it for about a year and read as much as I could. There is an assessment that you can take—one that I took—called the leadership circle profile, which is a measure of these stages. It is quite well researched and has a database of the results of close to a million executives around the world in some of our most important companies. When I took the survey, my score was eye opening for me. I always prided myself in being independent and creative in my thinking. What I found was that others saw me as more reactive, specifically in the core areas of protecting and controlling behaviors. I understood how this behavior was impacting those around me in my personal and professional life. I vowed to change it, to grow and to learn how to free myself from these inner bonds in order to bring my authentic self into the world. All of us strive to live our lives in mature, balanced, and creative ways, but clearly the reactive mind had its hold on me.

The second important element in considering the voices of the reactive mindset is the Jungian masculine archetypes. If you recall,

Four Archetypes of the Masculine Psyche

Mature Masculine Energy	Centered, Order, Integrity	Awareness, Insight, Alchemy	Mature Masculine Energy
Shadow Masculine Energy	Narcissistic, Tyrant, Weakness	Detached, Manipulative, Trickster	Shadow Masculine Energy
	KING 👑	🧙 MAGICIAN	
	WARRIOR ⚔	♥ LOVER	
Mature Masculine Energy	Commitment, Clarity, Action	Empathizing, Connectedness, Creativity	Mature Masculine Energy
Shadow Masculine Energy	Compulsive, Insecure, Destructive	Overly-sensitive, Boundaryless, Overwhelming	Shadow Masculine Energy

the shadow side of each of the four types represented powerful beliefs, tendencies, and voices that had captured control of our habits. Imagine how dominant that voice is when you are facing down a difficult situation. You are likely to forego any careful thinking on the part of your neocortex and to bypass your values and use the biggest sword that you have in your sack of weapons to address the issue at hand. (That issue at hand, remember, has the appearance of being dangerous and damaging to you and your ego and therefore demands this type of powerful response in this mindset framework.)

Let's take an example, where my inclination was to bring forth my shadow warrior archetype and in which I shifted my mindset and actions to the mature lover archetype. Teresa and I are trying to figure out where we want to spend the latter years of our life—specifically, to get away from the cold, dark New England winters, where we live most of the time. We usually discuss things very completely and have many criteria for our decision-making. It is also true that we have several areas of our life that, as with most couples, we see differently. Over the years, I have favored a Walden Pond–type of lifestyle and location, like our home in rural, northeastern Connecticut. Teresa favors more active communities, and friendships are very important to her. I suspect that this scenario is a bit like male–female polarities in nature.

My warrior voice, combined with my tendency to want to protect my safe space and privacy, reared its strong head as this discussion ensued. I could feel it in every fabric of my being, and I knew from experience that it could overwhelm and overcome me, and that it could hijack the conversation at any point if I wasn't careful. I could feel my blood pressure rise at even the mention of this discussion.

As I thought about it more and dipped into my inner values, it became clear that this conversation needed to honor both of our interests and needs. I am ten years older than Teresa, and it is likely that this decision will have much more of an impact on her when I am gone and she is alone. I wanted her to have a situation with community and like-minded people for her to bond with and to enrich her life at that stage of her life. I brought that voice into the forefront of my thinking and into our discussions. I went on record stating that I wanted that for her and us and that it was of greater importance in the larger scheme of things.

We have had many follow-up discussions and are still working through that conversation. I can still feel myself being pulled back into my reactive nature. My warrior wants to fight for what it wants only for itself. As you can see, the work is about bringing the voices into your awareness, then choosing the values you want to express and quieting those voices so that a higher reasoning can emerge. This is a good example of the pull–push that is happening much of the time in our lives, the dialogue within our inner self and the strong voices that seek to control us at all times.

Let's look at the voices of the reactive mindset in detail now to give you a chance to understand them and to figure out which are strong in your own inner self. After we do that, we will discuss some of the ways to deal with the voices and how to ultimately shift from a reactive mindset to a proactive or creative mindset in your life.

In what I am going to share with you next, you will find my distillation of a great deal of research. My hope is that by understanding the framework and the voices and their categories, you will be able to find your reactive voices and begin to trace where they come from and discover how you can work with them to find better methods of dealing with challenging interactions in your life. Later, we will work on finding proactive voices and bringing them into your repertoire to enhance your relationships and experience.

Table 4.1. Categories of the voices of the reactive mindset			
	Protecting	Controlling	Complying
Holding in	The hyper-independent	The victim	The passivist
Acting out	The critic	The perfectionist	The overly nice

Table 4.1 shows the general categories of the voices of the reactive mindset. These voices fall into two main groups: internal or external. The internally focused voices involve holding emotions or information in. Holding in means you keep the tendency or voice within yourself and don't act it out directly with and on another person. It doesn't mean that it won't come out or be acted out, just that it is mostly inside you. The other category is made up of acting out, which means that you verbalize the voice outwardly. It clearly has an internal component as well, but the end state is outward, with others, likely in a relationship.

The voices each have a purpose: protecting, controlling, or complying. These are macro patterns of our internal psyche that have emerged from our core issues, likely from childhood experiences. I have described to you that my core has resulted in more protective behaviors for me because my childhood experiences required me to develop behaviors to keep myself safe and in control of my life and destiny. Those behaviors were likely effective at that point and have been effective in my adult life, but they are now overused, and that is what needs to change.

Protective Voices

Protective behaviors do just that: They are designed to protect the person from perceived attacks or danger as experienced by the ego or the persona of the individual. We all are highly motivated to safeguard our self-image and keep our ego intact. When it becomes a full-out response pattern, that is going overboard, and it becomes all about safety and protection. People close down when this occurs and become highly defensive—even offensive.

THE CRITIC

The critic voice is a form of acting out and is all about keeping one safe by going on the attack, often preemptively, to get out ahead of the potential danger. This is a strategy that I employ way too often. It seems quite real to me; that is what I am experiencing, but as I often suggest, what you focus on grows in life, and if you focus on someone else's weaknesses, you will mainly see them in that way. Obviously, we all have positive and negative tendencies, and we would be much better off focusing on the positives.

Some of the behaviors that are hallmarks of the critic are being righteous or watchful, finding faults in others, undermining, judging, looking for things that are wrong or nitpicking, and picking fights to be right.

I can think of an example in my life a few years ago when a person on my team at work didn't do something at the level I wanted or hoped, and we had a conversation about it. The actions were difficult, and I should have been more empathic, but instead I attacked the person for all her problems and misgivings and did so in an aggressive manner mightily outweighing the actual problem, generalizing, and overall putting her down. I have felt awful about this over the years, but in the moment, my critic voice clearly hijacked the situation and my values. I am sure the critic looms large in each of us, but for some of us, it is a star character. Is that you?

THE HYPERINDEPENDENT

The hyperindependent is the internal voice in the protective dimension. It serves to protect us by keeping us focused internally and being so in control that everything becomes preemptive and leaves nothing to chance, totally protecting the ego from assault. *I have got this covered* and *I don't need anyone else to help me* are the frequent mantras of this voice. It is the taskmaster, the loner, the overachiever—all in an effort to protect the holder of this voice from the ever-present assault on the ego that we dread. These folks can also be restless and a bit ADD, always thinking about how to stay safe and ahead of the curve. Much of this dialogue happens inside the mind of the person, but the results are served up in actions and decisions.

Controlling Voices

The controlling dimension represents that part of us that identifies ourselves and our ego or worth by our capability to get results. A controlling person believes that his achievements define him. This type of voice will use power and will to create what they want, even at the expense of other people. This is about the will to win and succeed through perfection, a strong work ethic, and being in control at all costs. This externally validated sense of self-worth and security is as seen by others, and we must live up to those expectations to have the experience of safety and to feel worthy of someone else's love or admiration.

THE PERFECTIONIST

The perfectionist voice will have you stop at nothing to be successful. There is a hyper responsibility to be vigilant and achieve perfection. The individual may feel like they are not good enough and that this voice and the set of corresponding actions will validate his existence. This perfectionism can sap energy from others. Sometimes called a stickler for details, this person focuses on the little stuff that might seem less important to someone else, yet they can also be overly critical of themselves. It can involve compulsive thinking and can even be considered OCD when taken to an extreme. In reality, they are driven by avoiding failure and by seeking approval. As you might imagine, this voice is difficult to have and live with, and when acted out, it is hard to handle.

THE VICTIM

The victim thinks that everything is about him. There is a healthy dose of narcissism in this voice, as most everything centers around him. There is a hostility to the mindset as well, and it is sometimes referred to as a martyr complex. They seem to always be suffering in one way or another as they choose to sacrifice their life or face pain and suffering instead of giving up something that they hold sacred. In this sense, they seek to control others by having them focus on them. This is more of a holding-in type of mindset, as it happens in one's mind and makeup, but it is very much externalized to others. When you are within this voice, you are taking energy from others and shining the spotlight only on yourself, which is why this voice is a cornerstone for the controlling dimension.

Complying Voices

The complying dimension is a great deal about pleasing, belonging, and conforming. These voices seek to be accepted, and a good strategy to do this is to fit in and not make waves—in a sense, to be submissive to others. It is, in many ways, the opposite of the other two dimensions, but it is motivated by similar core issues—being safe and keeping one's self-worth intact. The person who is of a compliant mindset will often do this by being nice to others, even if they feel differently, and may attack them behind their back. This voice seeks to be good and worthwhile because of their kindness and care about others. The thought process is *If I am liked and respected then I have more self-worth*. In reality, these folks are giving away their power.

THE PASSIVIST

The passivist voice avoids confrontation, is tentative, withdraws to keep safe, and is also often seen as aloof. You might think of this voice as a dodger—someone who dodges responses, interactions, and decisions so that they will not offend. The inner voice dialogue might sound like this if we could listen in: *I am going to go along with the crowd, not make waves, and lie low in hopes that I can blend into the background.*

THE OVERLY NICE

This voice is often acting out as compliant, a flatterer, and a conformist. He is often seen as a sacrificial lamb or someone who is willing to do anything to be accepted. One might overcompensate with clingy and over-the-top behaviors with women. Often, they get stuck in the "friend zone" in relationships, using excessive kindness to make up for other things they feel they lack inside. Examples include being overly pleasing, complimenting and being polite, wining and dining women, opening doors, being very patient, and being a pleaser. While there is nothing inherently wrong with this, the voice has a sinister motive inside. That motive is to be liked, to enhance an ego that is fragile, and this strategy is designed to mask that by getting folks to like him. I have been accused of this by one of my sisters-in-law whom I often compliment about what she is wearing or how she looks. Although it seems to me to be an honest comment—and I believe it is true—I can't help but think that in some way deep inside me it is designed to draw her nearer to me or for her to like me. I do notice this is a pattern for me. I know men who are the opposite and strongly committed to bone-chilling honesty at all cost. That seems scary to me.

The main heading of this section could be "How Are You Hiding Your True Self?" The voices are mindsets that originate in our core issues, which power our behaviors, often without us being aware. We do use the voices to feel safer, more loved, and appreciated. They are strategies we learned from our younger years that have evolved but not matured.

Heuristics

There is a great deal of important research into the hidden traps in decision-making and thinking called *heuristics*. They are mental short-cuts that hijack our thinking to help us go faster in living our lives. They have seemingly good intentions but are dangerous traps that can push us to make bad decisions. In his *New York Times* bestselling book, Daniel Kahneman, who won the Nobel Prize in economics for his work, brings this to light. The traps are things like anchoring, where we give disproportionate weight to the information we have been given first or that is in our head. An example of this would be to mention an article in a newspaper about a trend before going into a meeting to make a big decision. One of the most powerful traps is the confirming evidence trap, which propels us to be drawn to information that supports our subconscious inclinations and fears.

I will give you a good example of a decision that Teresa and I made about fifteen years ago that we have regretted hundreds of times and still do. It is a great example of the power of the voices of the reactive mindset and how they can hijack actions and decision-making. When Teresa and I got together after meeting in Atlanta over thirty years ago, we were trying to decide whether to live in Atlanta or Connecticut. Teresa had a career, many friends, and a lovely home, and she loved Atlanta. I was raised in Connecticut and seem to have the land in my bones, and I loved it there as well. In addition, Timo and Morgan, two children from my first marriage, lived with their birthmother, Thyrza, in Connecticut. After much processing, thought, and experimenting, we decided to move to Connecticut to be closer to the children, then ages fourteen and seven. We were with them each weekend and loved our time with them. Additionally, the management consulting firm I had started was in Hartford.

Once we had made that decision, we needed to find a house, and we looked for quite a while, perhaps viewing close to fifty homes in the Woodbury area. We ultimately found a hundred-and-fifty-year-old farmhouse and farm in our price range with a barn and a beautiful view of the Connecticut hills. We loved this home, and it came to be known as Hoopy Farm, a place of hope and happiness; our seven-year-old daughter, Morgan, named the farm. Our years there were happy and fulfilling in many ways.

We both continued to work in our consultant professions and thrived, but we traveled a great deal to clients each week, usually

Tuesday through Thursday, and had long weekends with the kids. After ten years or so, we began to tire of the winters and travel and thought about buying a small home in the South or the West for the warmer winter weather. We did find a place in Atlanta, where we still had many friends and family.

It was around this time that I was ending some work with a big, long-term client, and—as it goes in the life of a consultant—wondering where, when, and if the next client would emerge for me. This is about the time the voices of the reactive mindset start entering our story. Several long-term beliefs crept into my mind, and the voices started taking over. Could I continue to be successful in my work, continue to bring in clients and keep my revenue at the level needed to support the two homes and the family? I still recall the fear, the concern, the urge to get ahead of this situation immediately to be sure that I wouldn't fail or be seen as a failure. If I dug even deeper, I could expose the lower concept, my core self-worth forever waning and my difficulty believing that I was smart enough to keep everything going.

It was then that the voices became even stronger, more powerful and prevalent. I began talking with Teresa about our situation as she was also slowing down in her traveling and consulting due to some medical issues. I can also recall that the confirming evidence heuristic I described previously started to take hold on my thinking and decision-making. I began to think that the market for selling our home would be best now and not in five or ten years. Little by little, the hidden traps of thinking built a strong case for me that it was time to sell the beloved farm, consolidate our investment, and find a smaller home in the Connecticut area.

When I get hell-bent on a decision, it is hard for anyone to change my thinking. Even though Teresa and I had many long and good conversations about the value of this decision, in the end, my fear-based thinking won out, I am sorry to say. We sold the farm to a wonderful family moving from California, and they still live there fifteen years later. We drive by it at times and lament our decision. It was our home and a place that our family loved. We loved to entertain others on the beautiful hilltop location.

Interestingly, fifteen years later, my consulting practice is booming, and I love my work and continue to thrive in this business. We have enjoyed the smaller home we bought, but it has not been in any way like Hoopy Farm. I can still feel and find myself listening to the voices inside my head that whisper the same things that came up those years ago. But now I am more aware of them and where they come from and am able to be more resourceful in making big decisions like selling the farm. It was a hard lesson, and I am sorry for it for myself and certainly for Teresa and our family.

Silencing the Voices

Drs. Hal and Sidra Stone have been the most influential thinkers in the area of voice dialogue in the past fifty years. Their thinking, called the psychology of selves, has been the cornerstone of my reading and understanding of this work. In that work, they describe many critical points. Here, I would like to outline a few that are powerful strategies to deal with the voices of the inner self.

The first is the notion that the voices are like real selves inside of us. They have a background, a purpose, a set of behaviors, and a real voice in our lives. There are two categories of voices, the voices of the disowned self and the voices of the primary self. The primary self is how we see ourselves and how we act in most situations. The most important part of this is to get to know these voices and to treat them as real parts of yourself. This self-awareness is critical to your management of them and to improving your effectiveness in life.

The second notion is that we must understand that we are dealing with opposite personalities and voices inside ourselves. The critic is not far away from the hurt, highly sensitive person inside you. You may have heard the expression that his strength is also his biggest weakness. I know, for me, that I can be hypervigilant and a perfectionist and can also be very careless and easygoing.

The strategy that is most useful is to cultivate the wise sage within yourself. When you feel in a bad place or do not know what to do, ask your wise sage to weigh in on the question or to help resolve a difficult feeling. Tapping into this voice and developing it inside you to both give advice and soothe you when you need help is very powerful. This would be akin to developing the voice of the creative or proactive mind that we spoke of earlier.

The last strategy I would like to share with you is another powerful idea that has its foundation in neurolinguistic programming. It is called anchoring. Essentially, you can anchor a stimulus and response pattern that is associated with a feeling in a triggering event. With the proper anchoring process, you can train yourself to respond differently to the voices of the reactive mind. A good example would be if you have difficulty getting up quickly to an alarm at 6:00 a.m. How might you retrain yourself to get up on time and be alert and ready to go? You might practice during the day: Relax and rest, then, when the alarm goes off, practice taking a deep breath, stretching, and being ready to go. You can use an external or internal cue to associate with the new feeling, like two taps on your ear to link getting up happy and fast with the alarm. You can condition yourself to not respond to your reactive voices, and you can also anchor the more creative positive thoughts and actions in their stead.

As we embark on our journey to a life well lived, the voices of the inner self loom large as a determinant of our behavior, our habits, and our life experience. The reactive mind is a powerful factor in our effectiveness—or our lack of it—in our lives. The impact of the triggering mechanism in hijacking our fullest, happiest, and most effective experiences in life is massive.

As we saw from the groundbreaking work of Daniel Kahneman on heuristics, we would do well to slow our minds down and bring the full brainpower of the highly evolved and underutilized neocortex into play, instead of our reactive mind and voices. The fight-or-flight response pattern is strong in men, as it is programmed from child-hood to protect us and our loved ones. But it can easily go astray, misguided by our maladaptive mindsets. We saw that there are strategies we can employ to both mitigate the less effective voices in our inner selves and to cultivate and evolve our creative and wise selves to come to the forefront in our lives. The improvement in these areas can have huge results for our resilience and well-being and, ultimately, for a life well lived.

CHAPTER 5

MOMENTS OF TRUTH

I can recall as a young boy being glued to the TV to see what Superman, the Man of Steel, was able to pull off to save either Lois Lane or the world. This attraction that men have to extreme power, toughness, being a savior, and perhaps being invincible is certainly a theme in the history of the masculine archetype and perhaps even an obsession.

This strength is traditionally oriented toward the physical and mental areas of our lives: a strong mind and a powerful body win the battle, make more money, and win in your quest for a desired relationship, or so it seems.

The *super man* of this book's vision is quite different, and includes a more holistic version that balances the masculine and feminine energies and gifts. This would likely include excellence and superpowers in the softer, more relational emotional intelligence, like self-awareness, self-regulation, empathy, and compassion, thereby broadening the list of the supermen on our radar to include men of true intelligence and service to the world. These are honorable men who exhibit true authentic leadership, who stand for causes, and who advance peace and love in our society and even the world.

One such person of the past century who would likely be on many lists of incredible people is Albert Einstein. As a scientist and a humanitarian, he was a shining light among men. He was a man of a single mold, a man of great integrity and brilliance, but what is less focused on about his life was his sense of humanity, humor, and love of people. It seems that there was no dividing line between his greatness and the many endeavors of his life. At a memorial service in Royce Hall at UCLA on May 22, 1955, Ernst Straus, his longtime friend and assistant, delivered the eulogy to a packed house. It is instructive to us that the opening salvo for this incredible man's life included the following story.

"Einstein had a genuine liking and respect for people. Often on our way to work he would stop to interact with people who merely wanted to be in his presence, and he always made time to find a meaningful topic that related to the other person or people." He strove to always treat people with respect and compassion. He was deeply connected with the spiritual world and was able to channel the wisdom of the ages to solve the problems of the universe.

What is relevant to us in this story is the fact that for all that Einstein contributed to the world, for all his brilliance and persistence, for all his humanitarian service, what was of note about him in this piece was his humanity; the posterboard for his life in his eulogy was how he related to others. We could then do well to ask and answer the following questions about our own life and legacy: What is it that I hope to be remembered for in my life? When I am eulogized, what qualities will be exemplary about me?

To further illustrate this point, let me share a brief story about one of my all-time favorite books by *New York Times* bestselling author and Stanford University psychologist Dr. Gay Hendricks. In his book *The Five Wishes,* he describes going to a cocktail gathering near his home and how he disliked events like this because of the small talk that often took place among attendees. He found himself leaning against a fireplace and his eyes met another man who was nearby.

He initiated a brief conversation with the man by saying, "I am not a big fan of these kind of events."

To his surprise, the other gentleman retorted, "Neither am I. I hate the small talk."

They were instantly willing to dig deeper with each other and decided that they would attempt to converse for a short time and see if they wanted to continue as an experiment. Dr. Hendricks' new friend then asked him a question that became the idea for his bestselling book: "If you were on your deathbed, and you were looking back over your life, and asked yourself what was unfinished or had not been addressed in your life that you absolutely would have wanted to complete or attend to, what would be on that list?" Hence the title of the book.

I would like you to think about that question now. What would be on that list of things that you would regret that you had not developed in yourself, discussed with another, shared with a loved one, and so on?

Having spent many years using this exercise with my clients, I can tell you that the list usually doesn't include all the beautiful places in the world or possessions or accomplishments. Rather, people focus on authentic actions, decisions, interactions, conversations, and possibly even evolving themselves to a deeper level of functioning in the world. Yes, the answer is different for each of us, but the themes are apparent. There are feelings that we have that we often do not express, feelings that are beautiful, sincere, loving, and compassionate. It is not entirely clear why we don't feel comfortable sharing those ideas or feelings, or why we just don't get around to it.

My list contains things like this:

· I would regret not having looked deeply into my life to evolve myself to the fullest, and not having confronted and defeated my inner demons.

· I would regret that I had not experienced unconditional love in my life.

· I would regret if I had not written a book like this about my journey and the journey that is possible for me in their lives.

· I would regret if I had not attempted to become the best husband, friend, father, and professional in my field. I would regret not having confronted myself, taken myself outside of my comfort zone, and truly tried to become the person I want to be in my greatest intentions.

· I would regret if I was not at peace with the manner in which I had lived my life and at peace with others in my life and my relationship with them.

Real life is lived in the most minute thoughts, actions, decisions, interactions, words shared, gifts given, and love expressed. These moments of truth are before us many times a day, and how we choose to play them out is what our life becomes. Our legacy, as we saw in the eulogy of Einstein or from our deathbed and the Five Wishes, becomes not about accomplishments or degrees, winning or losing, succeeding or failing, but rather the part of life where love and connection, authenticity and accountability and reverence and respect intersect. Those moments either come before us—met or unmet—or we choose to create them and fulfill our greatest hopes. Our lives are ultimately measured by these moments of truth.

The average human being has eighty thousand thoughts in a day, and of those, approximately 1 percent are new. We mostly run the same programs in our well-grooved operating system to produce the same results—whether they are useful, loving, kind, effective, or not. I would like to raise my percentage of new thinking, I would like to allow the positive, creative, and proactive beliefs to be the primary focus of my life. I would like to significantly raise my batting average as it relates to thoughtful connections with others that I encounter each day. This is the opportunity that lies ahead for me and for you in the journey to a life well lived, so let's dig deeper into the essence and practice, the art and science of these vastly important moments of truth.

Three Origins of the Concept

There are three sources of this idea from my own background starting over forty years ago that are the genesis of my thinking about this idea of moments of truth and its importance as a tool in the day-to-day actions of my/our lives. The first connection that I had with this topic came at a hugely mind-opening part of my life. In the early 1970s, I was getting a master's degree in counseling psychology at Fairfield University when in a course called Counseling Psychology 101, the professor assigned several books to help us formulate our philosophy of life. It makes sense that to become a good therapist one should have a point of departure in one's own thinking about life.

One of the books that we read was called *Man's Search for Meaning* by the Austrian psychiatrist Dr. Viktor Frankl. He wrote about his and others' experiences during his encampment in a Nazi concentration camp in Germany in WW2. The theme I recall that riveted my life and experience was this: Another person can do awful things to you and others. They can torture you, both psychologically and physically, and take away all your earthly belongings. But they cannot take away a person's dignity, free will, or choice about life and one's own self-respect. That is only yours to give or hold dearly to in life. Those choices are inside our minds and are a part of our beliefs and mindset. It is the basic notion of living our life in these moments of truth that defines us and our lives.

This powerful reading and teaching changed me in so many ways as a young man. I had been through so much of my own "concentration camp" as I referred to it with my mother at the helm as a child, teen, and young man. At that point in my life, I was still in the throngs of the web that she created. I was fighting hard to escape that situation, but in so doing, I was also escaping myself. I had lost my own sense of self—in fact, I had most likely never found it.

I had made many difficult choices to free myself, and it was hard. I also felt terribly guilty that my mom was so tormented, and I seemed to offer her such little solace as I was focused on how she made me feel. I felt guilty about my dad who had to endure her domination, and I couldn't do anything to change the situation. In a sense, I felt guilty about any choice I made for myself, and there were not that many. To use Frankl's words, I was giving myself to my capturer. It was the opposite of what he taught in his logotherapy, which he developed to help others live by his philosophy. His ideas are quite similar to what we learned from Kegan's adult stages of development, especially the self-authoring stage of maturity that so few from the research were able to achieve.

I first heard the expression "moments of truth" when reading about CEO Jan Carlzon, then head of Scandinavian Airlines, when he wrote about their epic customer service culture initiative where he met with five thousand of his employees in an airport hangar to describe how in the course of one day, there were hundreds of moments of truth that each person had with customers and that those moments defined the brand and how people saw and responded to the airline. It later became known as the Loyalty Effect and was written about in an epic book of the same name by Frederick Reichheld.

I have always felt that this notion was a powerful one in thinking about how a business is operated or a life is lived. The idea that all the preparation, teaching, learning, support systems, and resources invested would ultimately come to rest on a moment—an interaction between two people that would define the image of that company to its customer—was a powerful concept. The other critical element that adds power to this equation is how much ultimate success is defined by the mindset, beliefs, and feelings of the individual employee at that moment and leading up to it.

Making the link to the living of life and the moment-to-moment interactions defining our journey became a focus of mine. It was about that time that I came across the third and defining experience that solidified my thinking about this idea. In the early 1990s, I was working with the CEO of the Emory Healthcare Children's Hospital, Alan Guyer. Alan was a former McKinsey partner, and when he became CEO he hired me as a consultant to help him in the overall transformation of the hospital services and structure. We came across a book that Alan thought would be important to consider in our quest. The book was *The 7 Habits of Highly Effective People* by Stephen Covey. The book became a huge bestseller around the world. I was so impressed with its content that I decided to go to Provo, Utah, to visit the headquarters of the company that Stephen had created, the Covey Leadership Center, and discuss the work and how I might get involved.

Did I ever get involved in this incredible, life-changing work! I spent the next ten years as a primary consultant to the center and to Stephen, working to create a principle-centered leadership process inside some of the most influential organizations in the world. Additionally, I taught this material to executives. Most importantly, Teresa, who also was teaching this material worldwide, and I vowed to live the principles from the book in our daily lives. It was an amazing time and experience in a living laboratory of life. One of the critical, if not *the* key concept that *7 Habits* taught was Habit 1: Be proactive. It was essentially the notion that we as individuals needed to be responsible for our actions. That meant if you were to break it down—as in, *able to respond*, that is—you have the ability to respond to any given stimulus based on your ability to do so. This notion was that of personal accountability and being in choice in one's life and that choice being based on values not feelings.

It was a mindset and a paradigm about life that changed everything about how one approached life and made choices. It was based on several key elements to create a cohesive system of behavior, and that system begins with the most basic of all elements of human interaction and decision-making: reacting to a stimulus.

A Reactive Response Pattern

The first element was the idea that when a stimulus is presented in our lives it might trigger a feeling, which would result in a knee-jerk response. Figure 5.1 illustrates the notion of a reactive response pattern.

Moments of Truth

stimulus response

Figure 5.1

In this situation, there is little space between the stimulus, or presenting situation, and one's response. They are very close together and there is no room for thought between the two. That is what I mean by a knee-jerk response pattern. That response pattern has been well-grooved over a lifetime of habit-forming thinking and beliefs, and it is supported by a lack of skill in the area required to alter that pattern.

A good example of this would be recently when Teresa shared how I could improve my vacuuming skills, which—no question—need work. This type of feedback or request brings forth in me an old feeling, which is not a good one. I can feel myself getting flush and the blood gets hot and so do I. It brings up feelings of not being good enough, of someone else controlling me, and of being watched over, thereby limiting my freedom. This set of elements is strongly related to my childhood feelings and conditions with respect to my mother. It seems to be stuck in my body, and I have developed a habit of letting it control me and my response. Perhaps you could relate to this and think of situations like this that trigger things in you? Also, you might think of where those patterns come from in you and what it feels like and how it causes you to behave in these situations. My behavior pattern was the opposite of *response-ability* that we discussed earlier.

97

Just to complete the idea that Dr. Covey presented in his Habit 2 formulation, he suggested that this reactivity, or reactive behavior pattern, could be replaced by a new paradigm, a different process, and driven by a time-tested principle. The principle is that we—no one else—are fully responsible and accountable for our behavior. The new paradigm would be that I could choose my response to any given situation, similar to what Dr. Frankl postulated. The process is that one would put a space between the stimulus and the response before responding, and that space would be informed by one's values and vision of life and relating.

The Choice Box

Between the stimulus and response is a space that I call the Choice Box. The Choice Box contains critical information, input, and potential guidance for you to process and use to make a decision. To be more effective in this moment of truth or interaction, three things would have to happen in a very short interval of time. You would need to:

- Be aware of what is happening and of your feelings or reaction.

- Slow your reaction to the flood of feelings, emotions, and physiological responses coursing through your body.

- Use your intelligence and human endowments that you have cultivated in your Choice Box to intervene in your usual response pattern.

The Choice Box

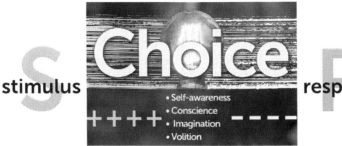

stimulus

• Self-awareness
• Conscience
• Imagination
• Volition

response

Figure 5.2

Let's take these three important elements one at a time to understand them fully. First, you would have to be aware of the feeling as it is paired with the situation or trigger and the ensuing opportunity to do something different. I call this awareness intelligence. Second, you would have to have the ability to stop your normal response pattern in its tracks, which is no small feat. As fire marshal, my dad would instruct grade-schoolers to stop, drop, and roll if they were to come in contact with fire. Stopping your normal response pattern is sort of like stop, drop, and roll; you stop your normal response, drop into another state of mind, and roll into your more effective manner of response. Third, you would have to put some other intelligence into the box to inform your decision and action other than the more common and comfortable habitual reaction or knee-jerk behavior. I call this choice intelligence. This other intelligence would likely come from vision, values, and using other skills like listening deeply. It implies that you have a set of tools or bag of tricks that you could dip into to pull from in any given situation that would expand your response pattern.

The Human Endowments

When noted author and business colleague of mine for twelve years Stephen Covey was alive, in his much-anticipated fireside chats around this topic, he would bring one other important notion into the conversation. It again has to do with choice intelligence. What might you put into the box instead of your typical habitual reactive response pattern? If we look more closely at this dynamic, we discover that the primary thing that separates us as humans from all other animals is the notion of what we could call human endowments. There are at least four human endowments we can focus on here as they relate to the Choice Box concept:

- Self-awareness

- Conscience

- Imagination

- Volition

Self-awareness, which I already mentioned, could also be coined self-knowledge or the ability to see or foresee into ourselves and our behavior or feelings. This is obviously the most powerful lever in change; without it nothing else happens.

Conscience is the next one. This is our ability to know the difference between right and wrong. To be in touch with our values and principles in life. It assumes that we have cultivated these values and have a high regard for them.

Imagination is the third endowment. This is our creative ability to come up with different responses, to vary our behavior for any given situation. Once again it assumes that one has thought about this and cultivated these habits before. A good example of this would be the notion I discussed earlier of skills or attributes for the journey.

The last is volition or independent will. This is the ability we have in fact to choose our response pattern and not be at the mercy of our feelings. These muscles are hard to develop in ourselves. Doing so is time well spent.

Change in the Moment

One of the things that you may have noticed or realized by now is that to live your life differently and change for the good for yourself and others, you will likely need to alter your behavior patterns or habits. That is especially true for patterns that are less effective and are coming from a place of anger, fear, or sadness and that propel you to bring forth the reactive behavior tendencies of protecting, controlling, and complying that we discussed earlier. It is also true that you can change and improve by focusing on positive things to bring into your life that are new and add value. To do either of these two strategies for change, you would need to be able to slow your brain/mind down so that it is not working quite so fast. When it is working fast, we tend to act more unconsciously and will dip back into our old comfortable but less effective patterns of behavior.

The greatest change you can make in yourself is in real time, in that moment in time that has the potential of changing everything—one thought, one decision or action, one personal interaction at a time. I find this an empowering thought.

After reflecting one morning on an interaction we'd had the day before, I shared with Teresa that I had come to the realization that many of these such interactions that I have with her could be construed as patterns of abuse on my part. In examining myself closely, it had become clear to me. I am aware of the anger and frustration inside me, and I know it comes out in a strong verbal manner and that pattern can be scary to her or anyone. I found myself even fearful of using the word "abuse" in describing myself. Doing so had a big impact, and she thanked me for sharing the insight. I think putting this on the table for both of us was an important thing. I know that after that moment and reflection, I have changed my behavior patterns and am softening and slowing my response pattern, just as we have been discussing.

Harnessing Moments of Truth

The moments of truth system hinges on several key elements. Let's review them briefly, and then I will introduce a new idea that is critical to applying the moments of truth process.

The first element is the critical notion that we have choice. Our behavior seems determined or programmed, and we have choice in every situation we face, and it is in that choice that our effect and effectiveness is determined. Teresa's mom, the late and greatest mother-in-law ever, Barbara Bailey, would talk about her value and ability each day to get up and vote about how she wanted to be that day. Voting is another way of thinking about operating in alignment with your values that you have carefully placed in your Choice Box.

The second critical element is self-awareness. This involves your ability to have enough awareness to be able to stop your less conscious and most likely less effective behavior, and to insert another behavior or action. I called it your awareness intelligence, and it is similar to overall emotional intelligence.

The third ingredient for success in the moment of truth is your vision of how you can be in that moment in that situation. If you recall, vision is a combination of your values that you have cultivated and become more in touch with in your life and your ability to exercise the human endowments.

The final aspect is choice intelligence. This allows you to purposely choose a different behavior, decision, or action that is more aligned with your values and is likely to get a more effective result in this situation.

The Anatomy of a Trigger Event

If you recall, a trigger is a term that is used in neuroscience and natural language processing to describe a situation or event that activates a reaction, most likely a feeling inside you. That feeling if you traced it back in your life, would likely be tethered to a trauma or highly affective situation that caused you fear of anxiety. Over time many things might trigger the same feeling, because the feeling is anchored in the connection to an experience. The core issue or central activating event is one of several that has been in your body for many years, and keeps creeping out when it feels that same feeling, even if the situation is not really dangerous. We are still programmed to either fight or flee from the old (reptilian) brain's desire to keep us safe from danger.

The stimulus box in the Choice Box graphic is essentially that triggering event. When it trips a core issue or reoccurring one, it quickly and unconsciously moves us into a reactive state. When this is our usual MO, we show up mostly in stage 3 of Kegan's adult development. The choices that come up in situations like this are the same two—either blow up like a volcano in reaction to the perceived fear, discomfort, or irritation, or zip it up and flee the situation. Most men have a predisposition to do one or the other. Dr. Terry Real writes about this in his bestselling book about the psychological origins of masculine behavior, and it is emphasized in his catchy title: *I Don't Want to Talk about It.*

Let me share a situation that unfolded for Teresa and me recently to add color to this explanation. I call it the Sourdough Bread Gratitude Story. We love and are very close to in many ways our dear friends of many years Jillian and Ben. During the pandemic, like many folks did, Ben took a liking to baking sourdough bread. Weekly, he would text me that a loaf was out of the oven and asked if I would like some of it. The bread was fantastic, and I of course loved it and really came to appreciate our connection through the giving and receiving.

Seems like a good story, right? Here is where it gets sticky. Teresa was brought up in the South and was taught from a young age to be very thoughtful and appreciative, even quite formal about that appreciation. It is in her DNA, and I love her for that. I however was not brought up that way, quite the opposite in fact. My mom was very suspicious of anyone doing anything for us, and she believed that it was not a good idea to let someone "get in your pocket," meaning you shouldn't owe anyone anything or they would take advantage of you in the end.

Perhaps you can see how this is going to turn out. Because of Teresa's need to communicate her thankfulness several times over— let's say—a two- to three-week period, she would check with me frequently to ensure that I was thanking Ben for the bread multiple times. Her inner voice was advising her to do so, while my inner voice was telling me that thanking him once was enough. The first few times she asked, I could feel myself feeling uncomfortable. As the questions continued, they became a full-out triggering event. I was uncomfortable with the concept of being in this position with another man, and I also was not comfortable with her wanting me to do it her way, which I perceived as overly thankful. As with many simple things that generate feelings that seem to be an overreaction, the origin of this feeling is from a core wound or way of thinking that has evolved into something more important than it is or should be. The point is that it becomes complicated to understand and is blown out of proportion. I was uncomfortable with his gifts and with how Teresa wanted me to handle it.

Eventually, I blew like a volcano and shared my feelings and anger/frustration, and we didn't do so well in the conversation. I am sure Teresa's feelings were hurt and she felt I was operating in a manner that was not polite and certainly not the way she wanted to treat our dear friends. It would be hard to argue with that point of view, and I am feeling guilty and not great about sharing this and the way I felt. The point of the story is that it was a real feeling for me and got me into my reactive, protecting, and not-wanting-to-be-controlled inner self. When in that place, bad things happen.

What I am attempting to describe is the power of the triggering mechanism and how it is constructed from each person's perspective. There are often two opposite ways of looking at the world. A better approach would have been for me to take some of my own medicine and move through the three steps I laid out above. The point is that it all begins with self-awareness, taking stock in the situation, and bringing in choice, which if we can operate from a mature and loving space, can bring about amazing changes in our interactions and our overall effectiveness as a person.

To be able to change the way we change we need to have the capability to see and do things differently in these moments of truth. To navigate these moments more effectively—in addition to the awareness of this dynamic in our lives—we will need different and enhanced skills to regularly apply this critical behavioral strategy in our lives.

CHAPTER 6

INNER SKILLS

The path of life is challenging and filled with trial and error, but with a consciousness of learning and growth, we will recover from mistakes and ultimately grow in our effectiveness.

The journey to a life well lived will take you along a very imperfect path, meaning not a straight or controllable line. It will be filled with ups and downs, challenges, roadblocks, and setbacks that will have a real impact on your life and your psychological well-being. It will impact your ability to continue to navigate this journey. Many before us have taught that life success is not so much what happens to you but what you do with what happens to you, your resilience and ability to dust yourself off and try again. It is also important to remember what G.I. Joe taught us in his message at each show's end: Knowing is only half the battle. We have to start doing things differently to actually change. As we move into the skills needed for the journey, the focus will be on behavior change, building new skills, discovering new ways of doing things, and getting better results.

The next three chapters are critical in that journey as they are dedicated to upping your game. What better way to up your game than to work on adding new capabilities? If you don't continue to grow and develop, it will be difficult to keep up with the pace of change and respond to the opportunities that life presents you.

In this book, we are distinguishing inner from outer skills. Each is critical in our journey for different reasons. The outer skills are the outward facing personality and person we are to the world. People see us as our behaviors, not our intent. The actions we take, the decisions we make, the love we give all make us who we are, especially to others. The inner skills, however, are the internal rudder of the ship of our lives, the North Star that guides and shapes our every action. Let's call this the inner victory, or private thoughts. This aspect is about getting your own house in order first and foremost before you can be successful in the outer victory, or public interactions.

The most important part of this thinking, I believe, is that it very clearly outlines a pathway to success in our journey. The inner skills is where our work starts.

In her book *Steering by Sunlight*, bestselling author Martha Beck echoes this thinking as she challenges the reader to identify their North Star, the ultimate guidance system for the journey, especially in difficult terrain.

Even though this progression makes great sense, knowing is not always doing, and we humans tend to keep doing the same behaviors over and over again and hoping for different results.

Over the past thirty years in my reading, reflection, coaching, and teaching, I have found that the following six skills are highly correlated to success as relates to the inner beliefs, thought patterns, and decision criteria:

- Self-awareness
- Self-regulation
- Mindfulness
- Self-respect
- Your inner guidance system
- Growth mindset

SELF-AWARENESS

Self-awareness is, in my opinion, the key to improving our skills for the journey. It is one of the foundational elements of decades of work in the emotional intelligence field. Self-awareness is your ability to be aware of your feelings, what is happening outside of you with others, and the accuracy of your reading of situations and the impact of your behaviors. It is your ability and inclination to step back from your day-to-day, moment-to-moment actions and interactions and look at yourself hopefully and objectively, although that is a tall order for sure.

For a man, and certainly for myself, this skill does not come easily. I, for one, have constructed my self-image and ego over my life to cover up for and eject against feedback and major doses of cracks in my well-architected armor.

I am good with self-awareness in my own terms. When I am well-resourced I am more open to looking deeply and questioning things that have been opened up from meaningful conversations with significant and trusted people in my life. Most of the time others can see the real you, the vulnerable and less confident or awkward you. One time I asked my brother-in-law Rex for some feedback, and what he said to me really jarred me, yet it was, upon reflection, so very true and accurate. He shared some really positive things about me and our relationship and also shared that I was at times uncomfortable in situations and would often say something that was not entirely appropriate.

My self-perception is that I am very appropriate and that I strive to be buttoned up and my best in all situations. Yet I know that he was correct in my heart of hearts, and I still felt very uncomfortable with that feedback and perceived strike against my self-perception and my own self-awareness.

As men, we likely don't second-guess ourselves often and don't feel as comfortable exploring our feelings, nor do we even experience tentativeness often. My well-constructed habits and abilities have been honed over many years to be confident, determined, and independent. Self-awareness seems unnecessary and something that would break down that façade.

I am working hard to be more sensitive to others and self-aware and accepting that I may not be as smart and right as I think I am most of the time. Writing this book has been an amazing exercise in self-awareness as it has forced me to question every principle and value that I have adhered to over the years. That is for sure an incredible opportunity for humility and opening myself up to greater awareness and thereby greater learning and choices.

Self-awareness is the ability to see oneself clearly and objectively through reflection and introspection. Some of us have more of an inclination and ability to do the work to improve our self-awareness. Research indicates that 85 percent of people in a study of one thousand managers in corporations believed they were self-aware, yet, when verified by others in their networks, only 10–15 percent were actually designated by a group of close associates to be self-aware.

Self-awareness theory states that we are not our thoughts, that is, our behavior is not aligned with our thoughts nor do we often show up in the way that we see ourselves. It focuses on our inner selves, compared to a set of values and a standard of correctness that we create for ourselves.

There are really two critical questions that are relevant to our journey to a life well lived:

- How accurate is our assessment compared to the composite of people who know us well?
- Are we willing to do the work to change when we find out about the discrepancy between our view and the composite view of others?

The answer to the first question means we have to work to eliminate the barriers we all face to achieve accurate self-awareness, like closed-mindedness, bias from our own beliefs, giving ourselves a hall pass or an excuse for what we might have done, and a lack of mindfulness or simply not listening to what others say because we are too stubborn.

The second question turns out to be affected by our assessment of how much time and effort it would take to change or our probability of success. If the benefits outweigh the cost, we will take the plunge. If not, we will take a pass and continue the behavior patterns we are comfortable with.

The old adage that we judge others by their actions and ourselves by our intent is likely operative here. I know it often is true in my own inner musings. What would an effective play at this skill look like if it were done effectively? For starters, we stop and take the time to get our heads above water and look around from the whirl of the whitewater of the day-to-day events. Just taking a few deep breaths or stopping to close your eyes and think deeply about something or someone or some interaction is a start.

We might ask a few questions of ourselves like these:

- What just happened?
- What was my impact?
- What was my motivation?
- How did I come across?
- What might I have done differently?
- Where was I coming from?
- What were my hopes?
- What can I learn from this experience?
- What might I do differently in the future to be more consistent with my values and aspirational self?

A less effective approach would be to only look at your side of a situation or what harm or ill treatment someone else cast upon you. Being aware of what is going on inside you, your thoughts, feelings, emotions, desires, motives, etc., even when you are in the thick of it is difficult stuff. But taking the time to unpack an interaction an hour later or a day later is incredibly valuable and a great exercise in self-awareness.

Some of us have the ability and maturity to assess accurately and some of us do not. If you are less likely to have this ability, then it is critical that you engage others in the process of helping you get a handle on how you came across in a given situation and what might have been more effective. Getting others' perspectives on how you showed up in a given interaction is invaluable, and just the mere act of asking and really listening will be an incredible deposit in the relationship and trust between the two or more people involved. If you wanted to get even more specific feedback for developing your self-awareness, you might formulate specific questions like, "Did you see me being open to others ideas?" and, "Did I leave enough space for people to enter into the conversation?" These kinds of questions really help in your awareness and guide the feedback giver to give you high-definition, high-quality feedback.

I am one of those people who has a difficult time asking for and receiving feedback. I am not proud of that, and I imagine that those close to me or even business associates might hold back from engaging me in this way because they might sense my challenge. I am attempting to improve my self-awareness by opening to feedback from a small, trusted group of friends and associates.

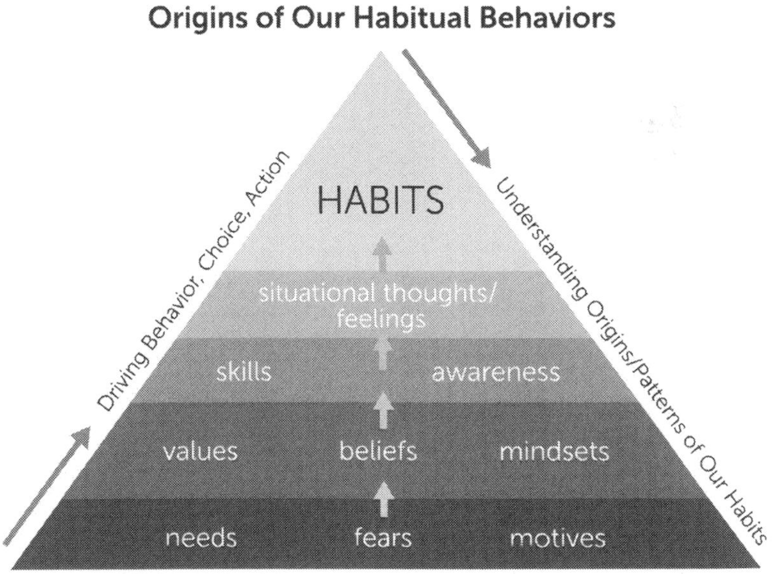

Origins of Our Habitual Behaviors

Figure 6.1

Here is an example of a situation that a client of mine experienced. Take a look at the behavior at the top of the triangle in Figure 6.1 and then trace down to the mindsets and skillsets to see where the origin of the issue lies. If you were self-aware, you might look into these inner spaces to understand more about the outer experience others have and the inner experience that is driving that set of behaviors or choices that you have made.

If you are so inclined to try and get better at this critical anchor to your emotional compass, the following practices might be helpful:

- Carve out space and time to reflect and be introspective about specific interactions.

- Pay attention to your inner state as you navigate challenging situations for a red flag and tag it for later review or ask another a question about that situation.

- Adopt a practice of journaling daily about what happens to you and how you feel and think about it and how you might improve.

- Ask for specific feedback and really listen objectively and thank the person for their thoughts.

I have carefully studied Daniel Goleman's cornerstone work and research on emotional intelligence, and my take on it is that the skill of self-awareness is the first and perhaps most critical. Without it, he says, we are trekking with blinders down the journey of our goal to a life well lived.

SELF-REGULATION

Self-regulation (SR) is the pivotal skill that allows you to stop and think about what path or decision you are taking and adjust or pivot to another more effective behavior or decision. Without awareness in the moment, or a commitment to sharpen one's acuity in this area, the hopes for change on the journey will surely be more difficult. It is the pivotal skill to kick-start the process of moving toward your new version and a life well lived. It is also true that without its partner skill, self-regulation, or as we might fondly call it, "putting a pause on the panic button," we are not going to get the value out of our self-awareness improvement. It is the one thing that is the most finite, micro, and behavioral that will make the biggest difference in getting your life on the track that you hope for.

Putting a pause on the panic button might seem to be overstating the case, but sometimes/many times it does feel like that is what it takes. Other times it's more like moving from being reactive in the moment to being more proactive. Reactivity is letting our triggered feelings and emotions hijack our response. When my big sister, Dolores, says I never call her or don't respect or love my only sister, and sends that guilt trip my way, I fly off the handle and get flustered. My blood pressure goes up, and I summon all the negative thoughts and emotions, pushbacks from over sixty years of this type of aggressive behavior, and I yell at her and lose control. Do I have a choice? Yes, and this behavior pattern is the one that I have cultivated and used to seemingly safeguard myself from this attack over many years. It has been learned, and if I am not very aware of myself and the situation, I will strike back. I'm not sure that there is any positive goal for doing this other than to address my internal anger and frustration with her and also the same behavior that my mom used to make me feel guilty.

In any case, I don't like it. I get angry, act out, and think in my heart of hearts that she deserves every bit of my rage that she is getting.

This behavior and the associated feelings and thoughts are totally in my circle of influence, meaning that I can choose to do and think about all of that totally differently, and have a different behavior come out the other end of that cycle.

Now is that easy or hard to do? Very hard, but very possible with the proper cultivation and activation of this new skill "muscle" called pause, or self-regulation.

Let's get into the science of this skill and then the artistry of it after that. Most of our behavior and thoughts—say eighty thousand thoughts in a day and perhaps hundreds of unplanned interactions— are fodder for change in this area. For many other interactions, where we do have the time and space to plan and anticipate our actions/ thoughts/behaviors, we might have a leg up on activation of our triggers and our responses, and we can rehearse the situation, which is very helpful.

Proactivity is often thought of as being out in front, preplanning and initiating things. With self-regulation, we do this with a higher degree of difficulty as it is in the moment when a habitual response pattern is activated. That response pattern or habit has a low probability of being the most thoughtful response. What if we could cultivate our inner self and subrogate our typical response pattern to a new, more effective pattern? In his book of the same title, Dr. Joe Dispenza refers to this idea as "breaking the habit of being yourself." My co-author Kendall Lyman and I referred to this idea in our previous book as "change the way you change." This cultivation of inner values and the human endowments is work that is to be done behind the scenes to build inner strength and an emotional compass capable of guiding your journey to a life well lived.

In order to pull this off in a moderate or even high-stakes situation, there would need to be motivation to change your behavior pattern. What is the bigger motivation burning inside you? What is that bigger *yes* for you? Is it your goal of being more thoughtful in relationships; more loving; keeping your blood pressure down; being a better leader, father, or friend; or is it doing the right thing and being a good person? Whatever it is, you need to develop and nurture this goal for your journey to your well-being and greater happiness and life fulfillment.

Research from the Full Circle Group longitudinal study over twenty-five years with close to one million subjects using the Leadership Circle Profile—a leadership effectiveness instrument used to help leaders become more effective in their lives and roles as leaders—indicates that 70 percent of men mostly are in a reactive state of being. This means that we are deeply entrenched in our stories, the self-preservation of our ego and our self-image, and our usual behavior patterns. That is the master that is being served by our lower, reactive selves. We call this living below the line. Living above the line would be more associated with the values, goals, and vision you have thought about and hoped for in this new journey phase.

Remember the Choice Box graphic from chapter 5? It is very relevant for this skill to be enacted in your life.

The Choice Box

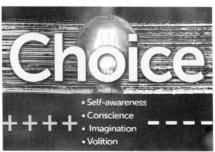

To summarize, there are essentially four components to put this approach into action in your day-to-day life:

- The declaration of standards or values
- Cultivating the motivation to begin to self-regulate your behavior in the most difficult situations
- Being able to monitor your behavior and get feedback
- Developing the willpower to self-regulate in the moments of challenge in your life

Perhaps the most critical element is realizing that you do have a choice, that you can choose to behave from above the line even in the most challenging situations. I call this CQ, or choice intelligence. It is the opposite of the stance that most people live by, which is more of a victim stance, in which situations or people or attitudes happen to you and you feel you have no control and no other choice than to be at their mercy, so you keep yourself safe and your ego intact by being aggressive and fighting harder.

The importance of emotional IQ has been documented widely as it relates to overall effectiveness and well-being. As it relates to SR, in order to even open the door to regulating emotions, one would have to be able to recognize emotions when they arise. When emotions like anger, sadness, and fear are at our doorstep, the physiology in our bodies changes, secreting hormones and other stimulants that activate our brain and body and motivate us to act quickly and decisively. Unfortunately, without regulation or awareness, we are doomed to succumb to those fears or negative emotions and strike out or back without real forethought from our neocortex, the thinking and rational part of our brain.

We might think about those reactions in terms of zones:

· Red Zone = high emotion

· Yellow Zone = frustration

· Green Zone = calm

· Blue Zone = thoughtful access of your highest potential and values

Just being aware of something incoming and our feelings is a good start. Cultivating our ability to move to green or blue will take some specific development.

In summary, SR is a key element in your journey to a life well lived. There are several keys to developing and applying it in your life. SR allows you to

· recognize emotions and situations that stimulate triggers;

· put space between your habitual reaction and your more proactive value-based action;

· activate the human endowments that define our
humanity; and

· be more in alignment with values, and have the discipline to
exercise that choice.

Our lives are built on the backs of our behaviors and choices, moment to moment, day to day, week to week, and year to year. Without SR we are destined to be in the doom loop or our reac-tive tendencies.

MINDFULNESS

The cultivation of a mindfulness practice allows us to slow our mind and be able to bring our life choices more in concert with our values. It is truly a skill, a combination of an awareness, motivation, and habit that with the proper training and knowledge can be developed and incorporated into day-to-day, moment-to-moment living to improve your well-being. It is a state of mind and a practice for a lifetime. As I have learned more about and practiced mindfulness over the years, I have come to realize the immense power that this mindset and practice have in determining my behavior moment to moment. When I am stressed, in my head, attached to my ego, less conscious, and unaware, my chances of being reactive, emotional, not curious, not synergistic, and small-minded increase tremendously.

Alternatively, when I am in a peaceful and calm mind, I am able to engage my neocortex and access my values and best thinking to add to the situation at hand. This is truly a moment of truth, where we are presented with a stimulus and our mindfulness quotient allows us to modulate the effectiveness of our behavior or thought as we access our most important values and principles of living and relating.

If it is true that this moment-to-moment action and reaction becomes the barometer of how we are seen and how we relate with others, then the lever of mindfulness is indeed one of the most important skills to cultivate on the journey to a life well lived.

Traditionally, mindfulness is seen and described as the ability to be present, to have presence in one's own life and in relationships. In a way, the word *construct* is counter intuitive as you might see it as referring to a full mind, when in fact it is the opposite of that, more of an empty mind. It seems that when our mind is full of chatter and things to do—challenging feelings and issues—we show up being distracted, not present. Think of the opposite of that, where your mind is fully attentive, but not distracted and fully present. You are able to be more conscious, aware of sensations, feelings, thoughts, aspects of your body that are being activated, and so on. You are in the moment, patient, letting go, non-striving, experiencing a beginner's mind, and you return to this place over and over again as your mind wants to wander. This experience requires you to be able to slow your mind, to achieve a slower brain wave pattern and access different parts of your brain. There is often a mental clarity and compassion that comes with this state. This aliveness is evident to others, and it presents an energy that can be experienced by others.

Not long ago, Teresa and I were walking the neighborhood streets of midtown Atlanta one spring day, and we ran into our friend Jeff. He said something to us, Teresa specifically, that I will never forget: "You sure seem to have your lights on!" Having your lights on is similar to mindfulness and being present, alive, and full of vitality.

Mindfulness is an outcome, a way of being that is the result of practices that slow the mind, deepen consciousness, and ultimately allow for greater presence. Meditation is one such practice that many associate with mindfulness. There are many forms of meditation that have been practiced over thousands of years in different religions, spiritual belief systems, and the healing arts. They each have unique elements, and yet they are all about the same central goal: to quiet the mind and alter brain wave patterns allowing for a state of being absent the buzz of the whitewater of our typical busy and less conscious lifestyle.

There are many forms of meditation that you might encounter as you think about bringing this practice into your life and learning. Some of those are loving kindness meditation, body scans, Zen, Transcendental, Kundalini, and basic breath meditations. Thich Nhat Hanh is thought to be an important figure in the modern meditation movements and has written numerous bestsellers on the subject. They all essentially take the person through a setup and gateway to deep relaxation without sleep and help them gain access to deeper parts of their being, brain, and collective consciousness.

I studied for two years with the Self Realization Fellowship, founded by Paramahansa Yogananda, who wrote a famous book: *Autobiography of a Yogi.* The book, which I read in my early forties, changed my life. It also set me on a path of meditation that I have practiced daily for the past thirty years. This practice has its origins in the Hindu tradition but is quite generic in its essence.

From a scientific angle, meditation serves to quiet the mind from distractions and thereby alter brain wave sequence and intensity. The usual brain wave patterning is measured in hertz, or Hz. Gamma waves operate at 38–42 Hz; Beta at 12–38 Hz; Alpha at 8–12 Hz; Theta at 3–8 Hz; and Delta at .5–3 Hz. A goal of meditation is to lower the brain wave activity speed from Gamma through Beta to Alpha and even lower levels. The quiet mind is functioning at this lower level during meditation if done properly and practiced regularly. These altered brain wave patterns allow us to access intelligences that we normally do not experience because of the preoccupation of the ego with anything but the present and the void of worries, feelings, and to-do lists. This twenty- to thirty-minute soothing of the mind allows us to regroup and tap into other sources of knowledge and wisdom that we normally bypass. For some examples of meditations that you can try, go to www.thejourneymanlife.com for resources and links.

We may also view meditation—or yoga for that matter—from a spiritual perspective. Many spiritual practices believe that when we quiet our mind and tap into these other brain wave speeds, we can access our greatest self, our deepest knowing, our most important values, and as Swiss psychologist Carl Jung suggested, our collective unconscious. There is a great deal written about this aspect if you are interested. It is quite fascinating and valuable.

My own practice over the past thirty years looks like this every morning: I spend perhaps fifteen minutes in initial meditation and quieting my mind through breath work, closing my eyes, being in a comfortable and warm position in total quiet or with some soothing meditative sounds playing softly. When ready, I begin saying in my mind a series of prayers, intentions, and my personal mission and values that I hope each day, each moment to be living. I call it my Loving Kindness Mantra, and you can find it on my website. It has been a very important aspect each day to reset me, remind me, and hopefully direct me to live by my values each moment at a time.

I then begin a deeper meditation, further quieting my mind through breathing and quiet darkness. I feel a deep peacefulness and teeter on the edge we call non-sleep deep rest. This lasts for thirty minutes at my best. I then think about my day, goals, values in action, and how I want to be and feel. I usually will read some inspirational books or poems and formulate a question or thought for the day to ponder about life and how I live it. Finally, I will journal for ten minutes about things I am grateful for and what I am wrestling with.

Certainly, I have noticed my feelings, balance, sense of peace, and perspective when I take the time to do this practice each morning. Meditation is like a habit or muscle such that when you use it and practice it with intention and acuity, it gets stronger and easier to access.

This can be a purely physical practice, with a focus on reducing stress. It can also be a mental practice to access different areas of the brain. It can also be a spiritual practice; you may even include your religion's values, prayers, or scripture to this time. The content you put in once the mind is quiet and you are at your peace is your choice and based on your unique beliefs. My practice is more of a Hindu or Buddhist origin, but I can surely see how reading scripture and meditating on messages would be very inspiring and guide one's life so beautifully.

Being Fully Present

The goal of mindfulness is to be fully present, to quiet the mind, to bring your greatest awareness and choice into any decision, interaction, or call to action in your life. There is as with most of these journey skills a deep inner guidance and cultivation and a powerful outward manifestation of that inner intention in your life. Mindfulness is a belief, a state of mind, a practice that enriches your emotional compass and allows you to chart your journey based on your best intentions and your fullest aliveness.

SELF-RESPECT

Indeed it would be difficult to discuss inner skills without considering perhaps one of the core elements of self: self-respect, sometimes also referred to as self-esteem. Self-respect is how we see ourselves, or the mirror of our lives. Our paradigm of ourselves as worthy or not has a huge impact on our outer behaviors. There is considerable research indicating that most abusive and aggressive behavior patterns have their genesis in low self-esteem.

I often refer to self-respect as the hole in my soul. It is deep inside, and I often keep it hidden from myself and others, but as with most things inside us it creeps out in many ways, especially under stress. I have spent my entire life partially motivated to shore up that hole in my quest for high achievement in my profession, sport, and personality. Sometimes it feels like I am in a race with that hole in my soul to counterattack it and get ahead of it so that I wouldn't have to see it at all.

I once had a deep conversation with one of my female business partners, a dear friend and a person whom I admired and revered as a consulting psychologist perhaps more than anyone else during that time in our company. At one of our monthly company team meetings, we went for a walk, and she shared with me that she suffered from imposter syndrome, a common fear that we are only acting as if we know what we are doing in work, relationships, or life. She questioned her worth and whether she was really adding value in the larger scheme of things.

I was indeed shocked that she felt that way. That is a good example of a manifestation of one's challenged self-worth. I know for me, this doesn't come up as much in my work as I feel quite confident and have received years of positive feedback from the marketplace and clients. Over time, it started to sink in and wedge into my sense of self that I was indeed doing my work well. I consider myself an overly sensitive man, and when I make a mistake I take it very hard. I suspect that comes from that same hole.

There is likely little question all of us suffer from a lack of self-respect and that it also has a big impact on our actions and decisions and interactions. We might then ask whether self-respect is a skill we can develop, since it is so deep within us. Nathaniel Brandon, in his bestselling book, *The Pillars of Self-Esteem,* outlines the following six behavioral strategies that will help shore up self-esteem.

- Focus on your purpose, values, and goals in life—your true superpowers. In so doing, you will stop comparing yourself to others and grow your influence over yourself and others.

- Exercise personal integrity in your life. Do what you say, and you will grow your confidence in your ability to deliver what you promise.

- Assert yourself in life. That means know what you prefer and need and honor it.

- Hold yourself accountable and responsible for the actual things that are yours to own.

- Accept your entire self; be yourself, and lose the denial and comparisons with others.

- Be a conscious learner, have an active and open mind to enrich yourself and gain confidence in yourself by growing and learning.

By focusing on and practicing each of these six pillars of self-esteem, you can take greater control of the inner feelings that are driving both maladaptive responses and also creating positive tendencies.

THE INNER GUIDANCE SYSTEM

One of the most important skills to cultivate in the journey is to tap into your internal guidance system, your North Star values for navigating the journey. Once you have the ability to quiet your mind and your reactions to events before you in the whitewater of day-to-day life, you'll need to reach into yourself and look for guidance. That guidance comes from your values, hopes, and the vision of your life that you have discovered for yourself. There are several ways that you can accomplish this.

First, get yourself into a relaxed and comfortable mindset, perhaps with your favorite contemplative music, a clear and rested mind, an open heart, and a blank journal page. Think about a beautiful tribute to yourself at your eightieth birthday celebration attended by friends and family who love and know you. Ask yourself as you picture each person standing up to share their view of your life as it was lived through your relationship with them, "What would I hope or want them to be saying about how I lived my life?" It is likely that the themes they share are things that are very important to you in your guidance system. Think about several influential people in your life, folks you admire and look up to. It might be a grandparent, a former boss, a clergyperson, or a friend. What did you value in them or what did they model in their life that mattered to you? Consider the roles that you play in your life as husband, father, son, friend, professional, community member, volunteer, etc., and write down your vision of those roles. What are your goals in those roles? How do you want to be seen by the other in each of these roles? Again, the answer to that question is great material for your values clarification. Finally, spend time in contemplation of your North Star at night. What is deep in your bones and heart that matters to you? What is your life mission and purpose? What are your values?

I have used this process, as have many people I know, to develop a life mission statement. You can draw it as an image, like a family crest, for example, that guides you day to day. I use my mission statement to chart my schedule and ensure I have scheduled time each week for my big rocks, the most important things in my life. It could be as simple as time to call a friend or having date night with a daughter or spouse. This is a powerful and simple notion to put first things first in your life and allows you weekly to truly live by your inner guidance system and develop new habits for the journey.

THE GROWTH MINDSET

We discussed earlier that beliefs are an important driver of behavior and habits. One of the most critical and well-researched beliefs or mindsets that has a significant impact on our well-being, our emotional compass, and ultimately having a well-lived life is the skill of the growth mindset. A growth mindset is an openness to learning combined with our belief that we can grow and change in our lives.

Perhaps we can start by looking at its opposite, as Carol Dweck, Stanford University psychologist and author of the national best-seller *Mindset: The New Psychology of Success,* suggests. The alter ego version of growth mindset turns out to be a fixed mindset. This belief is oriented around the notion that the world is pretty black and white, that things are as they are, change is unlikely, and you can't teach an old dog new tricks. This belief is represented by the idea that your intelligence is limited, and although you can learn new things, you can't change how intelligent you are. It looks at personal qualities and abilities as a zero-sum game: You are a certain kind of a person, and there is not much that can be done about that to change it. This system is guarded, fearful, protective, controlling, and likely complying as well. It is guided by a lack of comfort with moving away from comfortable things and ways of living your life. Imagine the impact of a fixed mindset on students, one's family and parenting, in relationships, and in business. It is the opposite of a love and appreciation for learning and growth. Our mindset has a strong correlation to success and accomplishment in the world.

On the other hand, a growth mindset is a belief and a passion for learning, an openness to new things, holding value for feedback, looking at things differently, being open to change, and constantly evolving and improving. The world is full of possibility from this angle. This orientation allows one to feel secure in looking at how things can always improve. Imagine the power of a parent or teacher or manager when approaching the world in this way to the student, child, or employee. Certainly, the culture of learning is key to success, but there are many other forces at play that are more energetic and transmitted through your voice, the images you share, the words you use that have a huge impact on your relationships and of course on your own well-being.

One classic psychological concept that I have always been intrigued by is known as the Pygmalion effect, or the self-fulfilling prophecy. In this classic story, described in a landmark HBR article entitled, "Pygmalion in Management," author J. Sterling Livingston uses the classic story of Eliza Doolittle in *My Fair Lady* to describe a young woman who has had a challenged life and is given great trust by another—her manager. She thrives and becomes a great version of herself through the positive intention and reflection of this important relationship. This extension of belief in another is as powerful as belief in ourselves, and that is the power of the growth mindset for our own continued quest to learn, grow, and find the best in ourselves.

I have had a bit of a love/hate relationship with this skill, but I seem to be making better progress in the past few years in opening myself up to this mindset. Teresa and I have a way of talking about this as we explore life and new domains. We call it "Teresa Time." She is quite proficient at this mindset, eternally open and curious about learning and trying new things. When we are on a car trip, I seem to be very focused on getting from point A to point B as straight and fast as we can. She, on the other hand, loves to kind of go with the flow and take a side road and stop in search of a new adventure along the way.

At first, I was so challenged by this approach that I was like a horse or cow, focused on getting to the barn as fast as I could, while she was, in my mind, delaying the accomplishment of our goal—classic overachieving male behavior mindset. Over time, I came to try out Teresa Time more and more and now even suggest it at times. Amazing findings and experiences have resulted from this mindset as well as just being more present in the moment.

I seem to be OK with a growth mindset, but only if it is in my comfort zone. I am much better at coaching my clients to be open than doing so myself. I know that feedback is tough for me as I am quite sensitive—perhaps overly so. Part of my overachieving is an attempt to get out ahead of my less-resolved, damaged self-image and fragility from a difficult childhood dynamic. I tend to get defensive and closed-minded, which is not my usual style, nor is it consistent with my values around growth and learning.

Teresa and I have had challenges in this area as it is such an important value for her. To think that her beloved would not be open to growth and change is inexcusable. She is right. I have learned that I am more likely to be open and have a growth mindset when it is my idea and I initiate it, and less likely to be interested or motivated to change when it is positioned as important based on the other person's needs or suggestion. I respond negatively more so to the idea of being controlled or dictated to by the other than to the core issue of being open to change. This is a work in progress for me for sure. What I do know is that a fixed mindset is not a good one to come from for learning, growth, and development, nor is it optimal for an effective relationship.

A growth mindset is not only an open mind but also a willingness and even a passion to push the envelope in even less comfortable ways.

Think about yourself and explore these questions:

- Am I confident enough and do I have a strong and mature enough self-concept such that I am open to another perspective?

- Am I open to feedback on my ideas, even when they are well-developed?

- Am I willing to appreciate someone else's thinking enough that I would even go out of my way to cajole them into sharing an opposing point of view?

Finally, I had the chance to work with a client in a big-box home improvement business that had been extremely successful for over fifty years. The arrival of Amazon was a huge disrupter to all competitors and had a huge impact on in-store sales and profits. The company had to totally rethink its strategy and found that it had many employees who had been trained and grooved in a fixed mindset to streamline the in-store sales process and the inventory management. It was extremely hard to think out of the box! Ultimately the company had to search for innovative ideas by having a large group of leaders focus only on the future, new ideas, and out-of-the-box thinking. They needed to utilize a growth mindset, a new skill for many. They were able to succeed, but it took several years and lots of learning and change. The old adage is so true that we become blind to our own thinking.

It is worth noting again here that the only way to change is to change! Change begins when you make a decision to do some things differently and most change begins inside your mind and heart. These skills are in your DNA and wanting and waiting to become part of your daily thinking and life, they only ask that you bring them forth and exercise them in your choices day to day.

CHAPTER 7

OUTER SKILLS

We have made a strong case in our discussion for the importance of the inner game in your journey to a well-lived life. Your behavior, habits, decisions, and interactions are driven by your mindset, by the beliefs and feelings that you have inside your mind. We could make a very strong case as well for the criticality of outside skills in changing your life. After all, your life is a series of moments of truth that are strung together and that produce a personality, a persona, and, in the end, a legacy for you.

The reward of your inner work to change your beliefs is seen by you and others in the way you ultimately behave in relation to the people in your life. We could say you bring your inner skills into the relational field, where you use your outer skills to interact with other people, small groups, family, loved ones, and work and volunteer teams. This is what and how people see in you as your inner life comes through you to give you a voice and an image in the world.

I have noticed in myself—and most likely you have also noticed in yourself—that my true self comes forth in these outer interactions.

We might think we can pull the wool over other people's eyes, as they say, but it is most likely that the true you will come forward, certainly under stress. As important as it is to cultivate a rich inner life, one filled with honesty, integrity, positivity, and vision, the skills that we use for relating to others occupy a huge piece of our success and well-being in our lives.

The key variable to be attuned to in this half of the skills is genuineness or authenticity. You can develop each of the six skills in this area like any other skill. As we have seen, the more you use it, correctly and authentically, the more it grows and develops. No doubt, you will need to open yourself to feedback to refine these skills, and you will stumble and then learn and get better at them if you keep at it. Find the meaning and value of operating this way in the world inside your heart, and the rest will follow.

Having a map and specific outer skills will support your journey, but there is one more important idea that might help motivate you to work in these outer skills. Earlier, I mentioned research from the field of neuroscience that indicates two important things that relate to the outer skills.

First, you can behave yourself into feeling. If you focus on the outer skills, you can, in fact, groove new neural pathways, and ultimately, the full learning loop comes into play. You will eventually start to feel differently and will notice more alignment between the inner and outer skills.

Second, you, as an individual, can work to change the world into a better place; this ability is entirely derived from the outer skills. How you model these behaviors and bring forth these inner skills becomes a model for others you love and our communities and society in general.

Indeed, the majority of my work as an organizational psychologist working with leaders in the great companies of our world has been in teaching and coaching them in this area of the outer skills. It makes a massive difference in the culture, impact, trust, and resulting success of a group of people working together to achieve true synergy and innovation. But it can also lead to crucial improvement in marriages, friendships, partnerships, and with family as you become a loving and growth-oriented entity. No doubt, we all want those things in our lives.

The six outer skills for our journey are these:

- Emotional acuity

- Opening to the other

- True dialogue

- Creating psychological safety

- Generativity

- Inclusivity

We are going to take a deep dive into these six outside skills for the journey, and it is important to understand that just knowing about them and their importance is not enough. When it comes to behaviors and habit change, you will not only need to understand these skills, but you will also need to have a plan with goals to develop these skills effectively.

Emotional Acuity

Emotional acuity is your ability to sense what is happening around you. This could be related to your own feelings and the feelings and emotions of others that you pick up on through nonverbal and verbal cues. Having a keen understanding of your own emotions and those of others with whom you relate daily is critical for a well-lived life. For most of us, emotions play a major role in living our lives and have a huge impact on happiness, success, and effectiveness.

Bestselling author, TED Talk phenomenon, and psychologist Brené Brown in her most-viewed TED talk, "The Power of Vulnerability," says that "the numbing of one feeling in one's life is akin to numbing all feelings." Men are good—really good—at numbing feelings. I am an expert at this and work hard at it all the time to my dismay. How about you? Recall our discussion of the universal wound that all men experience around five years old, when we learn that expressing feelings is taboo and dangerous for us. With that notion, we disconnect from our feelings, even though we still feel them. We stuff them inside to fester and build anger and resentment. That anger explodes outward like a volcano heating up its lava and spilling over onto a nearby village, or it explodes inside us, and we get cancer or depression. That happened to me.

With this tendency, you might imagine that our familiarity with emotions is low. It is very difficult for me to identify what I am feeling. I stuff my feelings and have always done so, which makes them hard to recognize. Around fifteen years ago, we found out that Teresa had breast cancer and would have to be treated, likely with surgery. I recall feeling numb about it for quite a while—not that I wasn't concerned about her; I just didn't know how to feel or what I was feeling. Then came the more detailed planning and actual time for the surgery. She decided to have a mastectomy at a New York hospital with a well-respected doctor in this field. Teresa is very close to her two sisters, Deb and Barb, and of course they were to come and be with us to support her leading up to, during, and after the surgery.

I remember feeling the anxiety rising as the date loomed closer. We had all trucked into the city, but I am not sure it all registered with me until the morning of the event. The three of us hugged Teresa and wished her well as they wheeled her off to the operating room. Not thirty seconds after the wheelchair turned the corner, I burst into uncontrollable sobbing. If you are a man, you know this doesn't happen very often in public.

Deb and Barb joined in the big tears, but mostly, they were consoling me in my feelings. Suddenly the magnitude of the situation hit me like a tidal wave. I was being flooded by likely months of pent-up, unknown, and unacknowledged feelings about my dear loving wife and the thought of losing her.

To me, that story is a great example of my own lack of emotional acuity. I was feeling something earlier but likely labeled it as general anxiety, not specific to this situation. I can only imagine how many times—likely hundreds or more—I have had something similar happen and was not aware, and the impact caught up with me later in more profound ways that had adverse consequences for my health and well-being.

One thing to give hope to these male tendencies is that I have become more aware of my feelings and the resulting emotions as I work on myself and write this book. It is like I am standing outside myself, looking down and observing, my wiser self seeing the situations and making better decisions. I hope that you can have that experience as well as you progress on your journey.

There are three thousand words in the English language related to feelings, and they are perhaps some of the least understood of all words for men. This lack of emotional acuity can be dangerous territory in both the short and the long term. Feelings that are not understood snowball into bigger things and may lead to inappropriate responses. An example might be when feeling bored turns to disgust, which turns to disregard and, ultimately, anger and acting on that anger. The entire logic train can be traced back to an unnoticed feeling of boredom and not knowing where it is coming from.

Another important aspect of emotional acuity is sensing what others are feeling around you. Men who struggle with this skill likely proceed in conversations or decision-making like they have blinders on and are unable to see what is happening around them. I remember reading about research that had been done in this area that really stuck with me over the years. It had to do with two types of individuals: field dependent and field independent people. Field dependent people look, listen, and interact with others based on reading the room, or being dependent on what is happening with others and asking questions or considering their feelings and thoughts. Field independent people are more insular and one dimensional in their view of things around them. It is like they cannot see what is happening around them. They only see their own feelings and thoughts. You might imagine the challenge that creates for others and the impact it can have on relationships and decision-making over time.

Albert Ellis, the founder of cognitive psychology and rational emotive therapy, offered up the ABC theory: A situation presents itself, a feeling is generated, and a behavior ensues. This is similar to the moments-of-truth Choice Box of reactive behavior. Understanding the logic of ABC is helpful, and altering that pattern requires reading the room and understanding your inner head space, taking a pause, and inserting values-based actions or behaviors instead of feelings-based misguided behaviors.

The final area of emotional acuity that is critical for our journey is sensing the emotions and feelings of another, acknowledging those feelings, validating them, and showing compassion and understanding for them. This is especially critical under stress or when we are feeling particularly vulnerable or attacked. Our interpretation of the situation might not be accurate; it is a good idea to validate it with others.

Opening to the Other

Openness is the ability to extend ourselves outward, to be vulnerable, to let go, to allow others' ideas to come forth. In doing this, we build trust and intimacy with the other person. It could also refer to the concept of having a beginner's mind.

Men are, by nature, more one-dimensional or singularly focused than women, I believe. I know, for myself, that my independence DNA intersects with my core issue of being successful and in charge in my life. This combination comes to me legitimately from the dynamics of my family and childhood experiences. No one is going to back Tony into a corner, to paraphrase a famous movie moment. The result is that, by nature, I want to be more considerate of others, but it is difficult for me, because my faulty belief system often over-rides this consideration to produce more closed thinking. I am often quite definitive, clear on what I want and need, and will advocate this position strongly. In business, this type of behavior is rewarded for men, and it has helped me in some ways to achieve what I have in my profession. I see now, as I look back, that this pattern has caused problems in many ways as well.

Opening to another is both a mindset and a behavior cluster. It looks like letting your guard down, letting go of positions, and going more with the flow. It means being curious, asking questions, seeking to understand the point of view of another person.

When I was teaching a course in organizational psychology in the MBA program at Georgia Tech, one of the case studies that I taught to the students was a great example of the impact of not opening up. I formed four teams of five students and gave them information on a company and three individuals to consider in the selection of a new CFO. They were to read the info, discuss it, and decide which candidate was best and then submit that to me along with the other teams' selections. What they didn't know was that two of the teams were asked to read the info first and make an individual decision about the candidate of choice, and the other two teams were asked not to make a decision on their own but to do so in the group, to come to consensus.

I conducted this experiment hundreds of times with MBA students and senior executives with the same surprising results. I called the teams that were asked to decide on their own first the advocacy groups, because they often advocated for their choice candidate. The other teams, which we called the inquiry teams, were to decide only by consensus. I did give some critical information in the handouts I gave the teams, but they were not on each participant's individual sheets; unless they were open to listening and asking, they would not learn this information.

The inquiry groups always reported a great conversation and a fun process, while the advocacy groups argued, defending their individual choices. Each time, the inquiry groups chose one candidate—always the same one. The advocacy teams chose a different person, but they also always chose the same candidate, even though the group participants were different every time. Being open to another is not just being nice, it is being smart and has major implications for success and well-being in many aspects of life.

At this point in my research, writing, and exploration of things that have the greatest potential to impact my life and well-being in a positive manner, I am very sure that opening to others is a central part of the journey.

True Dialogue

True or authentic dialogue is about becoming fluent in both talking and listening and in tracking others—what we call reciprocal nurturing. It necessitates the ability to let go, ask questions, and be curious, but also to be courageous in ensuring a point of view.

True dialogue is a little-utilized skill that has a huge impact on relationships and well-being. It is a conversation between two or more people where an exchange of ideas or opinions on a particular issue occurs. It suggests an interplay between the parties, skillful listening, empathy, understanding, and validation of others' points of view. Excellence in listening is about the connection between people. Ultimately your success in this area of relating lies in your ability to put yourself in the other person's place and to see things from their point of view—as well as your own. Hearing is not the same as listening in this manner. I have known few people who are working to create true dialogue in life; I do try hard to do this myself in my work and my relationships. I know I can do better for sure. Once I did get a piece of feedback from a client of mine, the CEO of a billion-dollar revenue technology company. After I had worked with his team for a year, he gave me a book with the inscription, "To Tony: The best listener that I ever heard!" I loved that, and it has been an inspiration to me since.

There are three subskills that enable true dialogue: reflecting, clarifying, and sharing.

Reflecting is the opposite of listening to respond. It is about withholding judgment and calming one's internal dialogue. You reflect what the other person says. This type of shadowing of another is empowering and relationship altering in and of itself when done authentically.

Clarifying is asking open-ended questions to get at the true and accurate meaning someone wants to convey, with the goal to advance the conversation. It is not questioning in a way that leads the witness to get the answer you wanted in the first place. Clarifying usually results in a deposit in the emotional bank account of the other person and builds trust.

Sharing is not dominating the interchange, but rather hopefully moving the conversation forward as you build on and link your thoughts and feelings with the other's opening thoughts. This turns light bulbs on in each person's head, and great synergy can emerge as well as a tighter connection between the two people.

One night, while I was writing about this segment, Teresa and I got together with our friends Bill and Joan to have a lovely dinner outside and a good dialogue. We were having a lovely exchange of thoughts and updates, and then the topic of different conversations came up. We thought that usually there were four possibilities for conversation among friends—or most anyone for that matter:

- discussion about other people and experiences;

- talking about what happened to us and what we have been up to lately;

- conversations about ideas that are emerging in each of our heads or that we might be reading about in the news or watching on Netflix; and

- deeper dialogue about feelings, challenges, learnings, and upcoming events that would benefit from real synergy and exploration.

This last category could also include our relationships and how we could improve them and deepen our friendship. I call this a meta-conversation, as it is about what is being talked about as if you were looking and observing from outside through a glass room with sound.

We wanted to take the conversations in our relationship to the next level, and we discussed how we might do that. I am hoping this will be instructive to you in your relating as well. Once there is an agreement, a level of trust and an inclination to dialogue in this way, the best way to get it started is to formulate and ask a question. Here is the one we used: "In our lives, what are we experiencing that is new for us, that is not an old story, one we have told many times?" When each of us shared, the others attempted to listen, validate, and witness the importance of the sharing and then and only then to build on it from their own perspective. Letting someone know that their vulnerable sharing had landed with the group is a critical step that is usually ignored, leaving folks hanging and wondering if what they said was appropriate.

When you can learn and deepen your skills in true dialogue, your relationships on the journey will reach a new plateau. Thanks to Joan and Bill, our skills and our friendship went up a solid notch that night, and we all left figuring out when we could do it next.

Psychological Safety

Psychological safety is the ability that we have as leaders and in personal dynamics with groups to set a climate, allowing for the member's best self to come forward and for them to be vulnerable. This necessitates us letting go of our ego, letting go of our posturing, and creating total safety for the participants.

The concept of psychological safety has come to the forefront of leaders and relationship thinkers in the past several years. Google did a multiyear study of hundreds of teams in their company, looking at performance and the level of engagement and trust among members. They found two variables that emerged to be the biggest differentiators among the top teams: the level of interaction between and among the members of the team, specifically the communication patterns not with the leader but with each team member, and the notion of safety, meaning a condition where the team members felt included, that it was safe to learn, that they were able to contribute, and that it was OK to challenge the status quo without fear of being marginalized or punished in any way.

Think about it: Of all the things that could have made a difference, these two variables stuck out. When you look at this, you might notice that they are conditions of the relationship between folks on the team and have to do with talking, listening, and subtle, nonverbal signals that are communicated among members. When this happens, people bring out their best.

Being aware of the dynamic of a group or even a one-on-one interaction is key. Sensing how people are feeling, reading the cues, and adjusting to the vibe is essential. To get the best in any relationship cultivating safety and trust is critical. Let's dig in a bit deeper to see how this happens and discuss how you can develop this skill.

A friend and colleague of mine, Dr. Tim Clarke, has done extensive research and development in this area, and he postulated four stages of psychological safety: inclusion safety, learner safety, contributor safety, and challenger safety. Tim describes these in detail and in a practical manner in his book *The Four Stages of Psychological Safety.*

Inclusion safety satisfies the human need to connect and belong. The need to connect is primarily experienced through talking and listening and feeling a part of a group. When this occurs, we can develop a sense of identity and shared meaning and the world opens up between us. The other byproduct of this is the diminishing of differences, bias, and false theories of superiority and elitism, all of which serve to separate rather than unite us.

Learner safety satisfies each of our needs to grow and improve. This usually happens though feedback, asking and answering questions, and making mistakes. When we do not feel safe, we shut down and this entire process goes dark. When we encourage and acknowledge people and ideas, we create learner safety.

Contributor safety is the motivation we have to make a difference. When we have psychological safety, we use our best selves, our energy, and enthusiasm and what we have learned to make our best contribution to the interaction or goal.

Challenger safety allows us to feel safe enough to challenge the status quo. Change is hard and requires great trust for people to feel safe enough to push back or extend, to put out a fringe idea that could be an incredible innovation.

Over the past several months, during the pandemic, our family was feeling the loss of regular visits and connection. We adopted a weekly 1.5-hour Zoom call to check in with each other and cultivate our relationships. It has been wildly successful, in part because we have been so intentional about it, but also because we created and discussed how to create intimacy and trust in the conversation that allowed each of us to show up, be present with each other, and build our connections.

I am not sure in the previous twenty-five years of our family time together on vacations or other events if we had this much safety and connection, and it is mostly related to how we built psychological safety. For me, I feel a great deal more comfortable in the family now as a result of these sessions, and I am feeling closer to each person as well. Overall, this contributes a great deal to my well-being and feeling connected to loved ones in my world.

Generativity

Generativity is the ability to see a third alternative, to adopt a win–win thought process. This requires systems thinking and thinking holistically about problems.

Generativity, as an outer skill for the journey, is usually the result of the development of the inner skills and the previous outer skills. It has several components that deserve discussion.

Generativity is the ability we have and can use to lead others and ourselves to be creative and resourceful, to solve problems and build trust. It is often associated with the seventh stage of psychosocial development in humans as was postulated by Erik Erickson in 1950, referring to the transformation of a person from an inward focus to an outward focus and in doing so helping others and advancing relationships and our society. It also refers to the ability of an ecosystem to produce new output, structure, or behavior without input from the originator of the system, as it is difficult to see problems with the same eyes that we had when the problem was first formed. Generativity can be seen as a concern for the future and nurturing the next generation. It is the opposite of stagnation. It is forward thinking and transformative in nature.

Can I make my life count? This is a question that generativity asks of us. Can I be a transition person in my life, transcending and jumping over and out of my own core issues, my prescribed persona, the challenges of my background and psycho-social DNA? Can I generate a new me, new qualities to relationships, new ways of relating to ideas and old paradigms?

To be generative means you have to get outside of yourself, your comfortable ways of experiencing or trekking the journey. The most powerful approach to achieving this is through the power of questions.

In modern society—and even in more ancient tribes and villages—
the community, the team, the village of fewer than a hundred people
is the main integrating vehicle to experience shared meaning, innovation, and collaboration across the needs of its multiple stakeholders
and members. Conversations become the primary vehicle to bring us
together toward that end, and many types of interaction exist. Those
forums can be on a continuum from more superficial to authentic
and generative in nature.

Appreciative inquiry is a strategic form of asking questions and
envisioning the future to build on the positive potential of a person.
We do this by discovering, dreaming, designing, and implementing
positive thoughts. In a way, it is the opposite of a focus on problems.
This approach is well researched and shifts the nature of conversations and reflection toward generative moments and stories when its
members were operating at their most creative and positive level. The
reflection and themes that emerge from appreciative inquiry questions are the starting point for the generation of the success factors
that are needed and possible for the team, relationship, or community to thrive. With that learning, we can leap over the old ways and
generate new structures, ideas, and ways of relating.

There has been a great deal of empirical research in this area.
One study that simply illustrates this idea, by Losada/Heaphy in the
American Behavioral Scientist Journal, outlined the impact of three
variables in groups of people relating together and their impact on
success, performance, and engagement:

· Inquiry versus advocacy

· Other versus self comments

· Positive versus negative comments

What they found was instructive for us in thinking about our relationships and generativity. The highest-performing groups had more positivity, more inquiry comments, and fewer self comments.

Shifting the balance of our paradigm and style of relating can have a huge impact if you are a leader of a team, a role model as a dad in your family, or aspiring to create more intimacy in your significant relationship. This is powerful medicine indeed.

Crafting and asking generative questions—and the hopefully big talk that ensues—has been both a hobby of mine in my personal life and relationships and a necessity as a consulting psychologist in my business helping leaders and teams to achieve excellence. You can grow this skill area by shifting your thinking in most situations from having answers to formulating questions that are thoughtful, positive, and generative in nature.

An example of this is a situation that came up for me just yesterday with one of my clients, a prestigious private boarding prep school in New England, when we were attempting to formulate an agenda for the leadership team's upcoming retreat. After getting a sense of the goals and needs of the situation, instead of spending time on my answers and suggestions for them in the session, I instead put my energy toward formulating five important questions:

- What is the role of this team in the school?

- What goals does it have for next school year to advance the school forward?

- How can the team best work together toward that end?

- How will we measure the success of the team in the end?

- How will we hold each other and the team accountable?

In most situations I face now, I approach either the relationship or the challenge with thoughtful questions that are inquiry based and positive and generative in nature. The result is greater engagement, better ideas, and more commitment to the end product. Generativity is indeed a critical skill to develop for the journey.

Inclusivity

Inclusivity is our ability to be fluid, quiet, and balanced, slowing down our decisions, distributing leadership, and creating shared leadership. It involves respecting all members' points of view and allowing synergy to take place.

Inclusivity is a powerful accelerant in relationships and the journey to a well-lived life. Many men surely battle with this, as we are acculturated to "go it alone," "man up," and "make it happen" on our own to show our prowess and strength. To be truly inclusive in life requires a maturity and strength of self and character. It requires a man to bypass the drive of the ego to be the superhero in every situation.

I will share a situation that happened not long ago in my extended family during a family vacation at our home in Connecticut. Teresa's sisters, Deb and Barb, and their significant others were coming for a week to vacation. The hope was that it would be a time of coming together and deepening our relationships. As you now know, I have a history of being challenged by family gatherings that date back to very difficult dynamics in my family of origin. Gatherings were quite scary and seemed unsafe psychological environments. I wanted either for them not to happen or for me to escape in some way, and I was motivated in those ways my whole life. Even though this family was a group of wonderful and skillful individuals, I still felt the anxiety of the past coming up for me. In the past, one of the ways that I found refuge was to focus on one-on-one time with each person to find a safe connection. One other related issue is that in the past, I have felt less comfortable and safe with the other males in the family.

In my escape pattern, I found comfort in heading off early in the morning with my brother-in-law Rex to play golf. We had done that for many years together, and I think it was helpful and fun for both of us, but, for me, it was really important to keep myself OK with the otherwise longer amounts of time with the overall group. In so doing, I left out Chuck, who was a new member of the family and someone I deeply respect and wanted to get to know better. I just had a hard time giving of myself, given the ongoing anxiety I often felt.

I later found out how much my lack of inclusivity hurt and puzzled Chuck, and I could totally understand his feelings. I was overly concerned with my own needs and bypassed his needs completely. This was a selfish act and a missed opportunity. We have talked about it since then, and I still need to work on it, as does Chuck. Both of us wanted it to be different, and with greater sensitivity and awareness of my behalf, that could have happened.

If you dissect that story what you find at its core is my lack of inclusivity. I was experiencing fear, isolation, and discomfort, and I took the path of least resistance in escaping from the authentic and transparent communication of my feelings. I opted for the easy way out and flew the coop to play golf—escaping, which is another of my coping strategies.

Inclusivity is a critical part of the journey. Without it, we are alone, stranded on an island. If our isolation continues, it often results in depression, the oppression of others, and a disconnection in relationships and, ultimately, with yourself.

Inclusion is a gift that we give to others. There are five ways that we can be more inclusive:

- Recognize your bias and concerns and break that pattern by articulating what is happening to the other. Be transparent and share your feelings.

- Amplify more voices, share more than one thought or voice with others. Provide context for other people about your inner feelings and concerns. Be honest and show courage.

- Promote accessibility to yourself. Reach out to the other person and make yourself available.

- Be mindful in your communication. Be mindful of tone, who you share with or not, and how you can be more emotionally intelligent to consider the needs of others.

- Be open-minded. Seek the ideas and opinions of others and see them as potential allies rather than enemies.

The behavior of inclusiveness matters because it is more effective and more considerate, and it shows respect and honors another person. In a marriage, inclusive means being considerate of your spouse, not only involving them in the good things but also sharing challenges. I know that I have a tendency to mask or hide or pull under the covers things that are challenging to others. I suppose I do this to not make waves or to be liked or not have to deal with adversity, but it causes more problems than the original issue. I am working to change this.

How about you? Where do you stand on inclusivity? Are you ready to reach out and bring people into your life instead of isolating yourself and trying to be a superhero on your own? In the end, being super at being a man and role model in our families and communities is more about working together than keeping apart.

Life is lived in definitive moments of thoughts, decisions, and interactions with others. These moments build our ultimate legacy and have a potentially transformative role in modeling these skills to others. Ultimately, in the larger scheme of our society, this transformation looms large for the critical role that men play in inventing the future. Investing in equipping yourself for this journey seems a small price to pay for such a huge prize.

CHAPTER 8

LASTING POSITIVE CHANGE

We are all travelers on the journey. We all have positive intention and want and even think we are doing the right thing most of the time. Yet we find ourselves in the white water of the day-to-day pressures and stresses of our daily lives and those currents push us in directions away from the path that is hoped for in our mind's best thinking. We are, in a sense, time travelers on this journey, and at times it all seems out of our control. Similarly, we can think about our journey using an ocean travel metaphor. Sea travel is dangerous and without anchor points to let us know where we are at all times. Like our lives, the ocean gets very tumultuous. For this reason, sea captains rely heavily on maps to navigate their journey in perilous sea conditions. Journeyman travelers must consider how they will navigate their own perilous life conditions. Answering these questions will help: What is my North Star to keep the focus in day-to-day life? How can I know what to change and how to change it to now and forever become the person that I desire to be? What is the map of that journey?

The journey of our lives is essentially a series of choices in key moments of truth. Unfortunately, the road that we sometimes take and the decisions that we make are not easily taken back. Unlike car travel on roads, when we take a wrong turn in life, we can't always so easily fix the mistake. However, when we make a choice along the path, those choices have major implications, and those decisions and impacts could take us further into a downward spiral that we may not be able to return from. Fortunately, if we are lucky and have a strong will, we can learn from our mistakes, make a conscious decision to take another road, travel at a slower pace, and even bring others along with us on the new road.

The critical nature of these journey choices necessitates a compass to keep us traveling to our true north. That true north represents our governing values, our sturdy vision, and our resolve to reach our destination as it is needed to stay the course in our lives.

This is for each and all of us a not-so-perfect path. It is not a straight line to a life well lived. As we learn, we keep moving forward, keep climbing the mountains that life presents. Some people are ahead of us on this ascent, some behind us, and some right alongside us. As we ascend and reach the peak of the mountain, we are able to see farther and with more clarity from this newly attained altitude. From that higher point, we see peaks that we have not seen before from the lower altitudes, and our vision of life expands. This process continues throughout our lives if we are on a conscious pathway. We keep learning, growing, discovering, and forging new paths, ever expanding on our vision.

The key thing to remember is that, unlike a rocket blasting off for Mars, where the major amount of energy needed is to break through gravity in the initial minutes, the opposite is true in deciding to make change in yourself. Figuring out what to change and getting motivated to do so is hard, but not anywhere near as hard as sustaining the change over time. Sustained change in any area of life is truly the holy grail of change.

For most people, the well-grooved and -oiled habitual pathways in the brain and in our habits take precedent in our daily behavioral choices. For most of us, we make and sustain only very few life changes that improve our life and its conditions. We need to make the best of those and to add to them as we learn how to navigate this critical part of the journey. Let's see if we can figure out how to overcome the typically low probabilities for sustained change and discover how we can achieve truly lasting change.

Steps on Our Journey

A question will continue to emerge in this journey: Have I arrived, and how will I know? The easy answer to that question is that we are always in the process, on the journey. I have found that I cannot take my focus off my process of evolving and transforming myself. It is way too easy to digress back to the norm or the more reactive habits formed over a lifetime. What becomes critical is to solidify and become disciplined to the process of change and growth for yourself. What follows is a process that includes twelve elements that can guide you through the change process. The steps are sequential in nature and in a sense like stage-gates where you need to step into and through each one in succession before you go to the next one. As you read through them, bring to mind your own issue, challenge, negative habit, or trait.

STEP 1: ADMIT YOUR CHALLENGE

We must admit we are powerless to control every aspect of our journey. This critical first step is often the hardest to take. To open up, to admit past defeat, and to suggest that we are not able to manage our challenges is huge. In the journeyman process, that would be akin to admitting that we are challenged. We are difficult to live with. We are even hurting others or maybe not loving them well. This is challenging because, unless we are at a crisis point, it is hard to muster up enough motivation to take even this first step. It takes an exceptionally strong person to do so based on a smaller life storm or even an aspirational vision.

STEP 2: LOOK BEYOND YOURSELF

When things are so difficult and we have tried our worldly powers and we still are not able to overcome our challenges, we have nowhere else to turn but to our creator. For the journeyman, this entails the acknowledgment that there is greater collective intelligence beyond our own small world and capabilities.

STEP 3: LET GO

We must let go of the maladaptive behavior patterns of the past. Doing so would allow us to be open to altering our belief systems to allow for learning and growth to emerge. This step is about locking in a partnership with someone or something other than just yourself.

STEP 4: TRULY ASSESS YOURSELF

For the journeyman, we must open ourselves up to the feedback of others. This will help us sharpen our sense of self-awareness to be able to look at ourselves through realistic and more hopeful eyes as well as through the eyes of our loved ones.

STEP 5: ADMIT YOUR MISTAKES

AA research suggests that admitting the exact nature of our wrongs is the most difficult step—and no wonder why! Thinking about our challenges and taking them on is hard enough, but to actually share them with another necessitates truly letting go of our ego and need for control.

STEP 6: EMBRACE CHANGE

You must commit. You must be all in on this goal to change. This is true commitment and conviction for the journeyman.

STEP 7: ASK FOR HELP

On our journey, we need help. We must humbly ask our support system to remove our shortcomings. We must continue to let go, ask for forgiveness, and support aspects of our lives that have gotten out of hand. You cannot change on your own.

STEP 8: LIST WHO YOU'VE HURT

Make a list of all the people you have harmed through your reactive mindset and be willing to apologize. This is such an important and difficult step. It means going public and sharing things that have been private or hidden in ourselves. This is both disarming and incredibly empowering in relationships. It is an ultimate act of humility and giving oneself to another. When I shared with Teresa recently that I felt I had been abusive to her verbally and mentally, it had a huge impact on her, and she told me so.

STEP 9: MAKE IT RIGHT

We must then be willing to make amends, to do what is necessary to set up time to discuss and share with others. This step makes our change journey very real, and it is an act of immense courage.

STEP 10: CONTINUE YOUR SELF-REFLECTION

Since our journey is a larger process over time, as we get to a higher peak and look out, we see things we have not seen before. We must own them and take them on in a similar manner as the past few steps. This is a lifelong process, not a one-time event or transaction.

STEP 11: CONTINUE GROWING

On the journey, we need to continue to cultivate our mind, our heart, and our soul through whatever methods work for us and our value system. For me, that is meditation and prayer. We must sustain a state of grace on our journey.

STEP 12: WAKE UP

For the larger journey and the journeyman, we are aiming for leadership of men's groups to facilitate this process in our world, much like AA members do in their meetings around the world. This is our gift. We have traveled in territory that is revered and needs to be shared with others. Waking up is the acknowledgment that you have been through this process and are awakened by this journey and are now in a revered position to help others on a similar journey.

When you view these steps, you can zoom out and see some very important themes for sustained commitment to change on the journey. One major theme is that when things get difficult and unmanageable we would do well to let go of control and admit that we need help. That help can come in many forms and that will emerge for the person who is open to change. An honest assessment of our situation is also critical; we have seen the power and necessity of a keen self-awareness throughout this book. One of the hardest and most impactful steps you can take is the sharing of your shortcomings with others, especially loved ones. It is very difficult to muster up the courage and humility to do so, but worth a great deal in the end. The notion of cultivating your mind and heart through meditation and prayer is also central to the journey.

Perhaps one of the most important elements in the success of AA over the years has been the group meetings, where members come together to witness and support their fellow brothers and sisters on the journey to sobriety. This social and psychological support is critical to sustained results, and we feel a connection to others and want to journey with them to a better place. The research we saw from the *Change or Die* book underlined the importance of the social aspect of learning and change. We not only need to commit to others our change intentions but we will also benefit greatly by going on the journey with them.

Three Paths to Travel

All in all, our journey, our quest to take on our challenges and achieve our vision of a better life, is well informed by the AA model of change. With that model as a backdrop, let's begin moving toward pulling together the main ideas of our discussion so far and see if we can assist you in developing a concrete plan to take the steps necessary to sustain the changes in your life you hope for on your journey. To do so, I am going to approach this task from three ways to accommodate varying learning and thinking styles and tap into your best mode of learning. The first is a story, the second is a formula, and the third is a holistic framework with a sequence of actions. Hopefully, you will be able to relate to one or more of these descriptions, and they will help kickstart your journey.

A STORY OF CHANGE

Toby was a thirty-nine-year-old man. He had done most all the right things in his life up to that point. He played sports growing up, performed well academically in high school and college, had strong friendships, was in good health, and did his share of partying. He married at twenty-five to a wonderful person; her name was Jenny. He started a career after going to law school, working for a regional law firm in the Northeast. Toby and Jenny bought a home, and over the next ten years had two children—a boy and a girl. They were relatively close to the families of origin for each of them, although there were challenging dynamics in both families to deal with for sure. Jenny was a great mom but also missed her art career, which was her passion; she really didn't have time to devote to this with the two kids in their lives. Things were going well for Toby in his professional life, and he made partner in the firm, which was taking him away from the family and Jenny increasingly over time. Work became most of his life, and yet he devoted whatever time he could to Jenny and the kids when he was not working.

When he turned thirty-eight, about thirteen years into the marriage, Toby started to feel trapped and uncomfortable, unfulfilled. He wasn't sure where that came from, but it was unsettling and starting to creep into his thoughts and decisions in his life. It was more about him and his independence than anything else. He started to party with people around business trips, and it was fun and energizing for him. He also knew it was potentially dangerous to his marriage, but it seemed like it was difficult to turn back at this point. He also felt the pang of not being trustworthy, which had always been a hallmark of his philosophy of life. Things started to go really fast, and actions and feelings began to multiply, and the trust and good feelings in the marriage began to crumble to a point from which it seemed it would be difficult to return.

There were many moments when Toby was torn about all of this, as was Jenny. He felt terribly guilty about what was happening, certainly as related to Jenny's feelings and of course the kids. Suffice to say things did fall apart and so did he as a result. He mostly felt tremendous guilt, remorse, sadness, and confusion about everything that happened and was still happening. He began seeing a therapist again, which he had initially started doing during the early challenges in the relationship. It was becoming clearer to him that core issues and the resulting maladaptive beliefs and behaviors were patterns in his life that were affecting his behavior patterns in personal and professional situations. These things were not going away, nor were they changing. They were having more and more impact on his life in ways that were seemingly out of his control.

With that basis of understanding of Toby's situation—probably not an unusual storyline in the chronicles of a man's journey—let us see what could have been done at various junctures on his life path. We will take a look at a point in time when he first started to feel unsettled, at age thirty-eight, and we will also look at what might happen at age forty-four, after the divorce, when he is looking to restart his life. These are both inflection points on the time map of his life when he could have made a courageous decision to stop the transmission of his core dynamic and faulty belief system and reach for a new way of living and being.

For a man on a conscious journey, this is a defining moment in life—the awareness and decision to make a change, to take himself on the journey, to achieve lasting sustaining change or to succumb to the voices inside him that are fear-based and emanating from his inner child wounds.

The first and most important step he could have taken was to tap into his self-awareness and to acknowledge—truly notice—and feel into the feelings of unease. That sentence deserves repeating. Please read it again! His choice was to override the feelings and take another route to his life decisions by numbing himself and choosing other behaviors to take him away from these feelings. For men, these feelings are directly linked to childhood trauma and the ensuing feelings of shame, guilt, fear, and anger. These feelings too often result in what psychologists call *covert depression*. While women are more likely to express their core issues and childhood trauma in an extroverted manner (depression, manic episodes, phobias, panic disorders), men tend to introvert those feelings (primarily through alcohol abuse and antisocial personality disorders), and that is where and how the condition of covert depression manifests itself.

Toby had many inner thoughts that he hardly understood, but overall, the mix of them in his mind and emotions resulted in an array of feelings, behaviors, and faulty beliefs about his situation. He didn't know how to deal with all this and wasn't about to talk about it with anyone. He stuffed it deep inside as most men choose to do.

When his feelings came knocking at his front door, he did not understand them, and the last thing he wanted to do was to discuss them with anyone, especially Jenny, so they remained unexpressed. This created a cycle of repressed feelings, which became a general numbness and with that, tension and stress built up inside of him, waiting to find a time to overreact, blow up/fight, run away, or act out in ways he was not proud of and that were not in keeping with his true nature.

The situation lasted for years, on and off, and eventually ate away at so many of the good parts of him that he was left with only his maladaptive behaviors to cope. His inner voices of the reactive mindset gradually took over his mind and resulted in more and more faulty beliefs and behaviors.

Needless to say, the situation did not resolve itself positively, and there was a great deal of pain for him, his wife, and the family with their divorce. He had major illness during that time as well, likely related to his covert depression.

Fortunately, he was able to remain highly functional at work, where he did get some positive ego building strokes from his peers and clients. He became more focused on his work almost as a getaway. We certainly see this with people who become workaholics.

If Toby had the wisdom of some of the insights from this book, what could he have done that might have diverted him from the path he took and the resulting impacts?

The choices Toby might have made could have looked something like this: If he had known about this dynamic in himself and could understand the feelings, identify them, acknowledge that they existed and were just feelings, just the mere act of feeling into them, perhaps talking about them with someone else, would have helped to move the energy and open him up to other possibilities.

One technique we have not discussed that is highly effective is energy release work. I have done this many times, and it is truly transformational. It is based on the notion that feelings are just energy and that energy can be moved through you and out of you. I have accomplished this by getting into a quiet, noise-resistant room and having a pillow or cushion handy. Feel the feelings, shout them out to the world in your loudest and most energetic voice. While you are doing this, beat the pillow with your hands or feet, anything to get the energy moving through you and out of you. I have experienced the energy dissipate as a result. This became a regular practice of mine over time to deal with rogue or more reoccurring feelings.

If Toby had known what covert depression symptoms look like, and that he was experiencing classic symptoms, he could have used short-term behavioral strategies and longer-term learning approaches to cope. I will describe several that are meant to quiet the saboteur voices and bring forward the sage or wise elder voices inside you.

The short-term approach is similar to the moments-of-truth approach, with some additional elements. I call that approach developing a relational operating system (ROS). The ROS is a self-management system to deal with the moments of feeling anger, sadness, fear, and guilt that fester over time. Instead of years of therapy to learn about how those feelings were generated in childhood, Toby would learn the proactive practice of reparenting himself in that moment of truth. He might deeply inhale and exhale to center himself and remind himself that he is not a child experiencing these feelings but an adult in his late thirties. By summoning his inner sage to soothe and calm his thoughts, he could address the reoccurring issues of feeling trapped and out of control. He could say *no* to the voices of the reactive mindset that summon him yet again, and *yes* to the mature man inside who is fully capable of navigating this storm of feelings.

The longer-term approach would involve the cultivation of mindfulness practices like meditation and breathing to calm the mind and allow the four human endowments we discussed earlier to come forth and be more involved in the decisions about how to proceed. By slowing the mind, we engage our neocortex, the thinking part of our brain to summon its wise counsel. We also say no to the trigger-happy amygdala part of our brain that is mainly reactive to perceived threats and engages the flight-or-fight responses.

Ultimately, learning this internal technology of proactively approaching these feelings and situations in these practical ways becomes a learned skill for Toby to acquire and develop over time. This approach is more like building a skill, coaching yourself through that skill on a daily and weekly basis, and retooling yourself to deal with these deep-seated older feelings and the resulting behavior patterns. Think of this as a redesign of your life operating system that has the potential to change your life. As a man wanting a concrete and practical approach to change, this hands-on approach is preferred and has worked for me in my own journey to greater effectiveness and peace in my life. Hopefully you will have a similar experience.

Therapy is of course extremely useful if you are interested in understanding the dynamic from your family of origin. This understanding creates additional insight and could have been a great motivation for Toby as well.

The other inflection point in time would be Toby at age forty-four years, after all of this happened and things settled down for him in his life. He could have learned about the dynamics at play, and the internal technology and other strategies to deal with the feelings as they occur. Over time he would learn how to cultivate the short-term and longer-term strategies for coping, apply those skills proactively outside of a high-stress confrontation, and change his behavior patterns. If he did not do this, he would likely repeat the pattern again in relating to others in differing relationships. This is what I described in chapter 3, when I noticed that "wherever I went in life, there I was again," meaning that the situation had changed, but I hadn't. I was the same person with the same behavior patterns, so I got the same results. The approach is akin to hiding one's head in the sand, and it's what some call the definition of insanity: continuing the same behaviors while hoping for different results.

A CHANGE STRATEGY FORMULA

The second approach to creating lasting positive change in negative behavior patterns is a simple and logical formula. It looks something like this:

$$\text{change strategy} = A + I + CA + AAR$$

The following is an explanation of a change strategy for lasting positive change. Effective change is equal to a clear, honest, and accurate assessment (A) of the situation. That would include your feelings, your beliefs about the situation, your resulting behaviors, and the impact both short and long term on your well-being and relationships. One question we need to address is how you could conduct such an effective and meaningful assessment.

The *I* stands for insight into the root cause of the feelings, beliefs, and behaviors. We can do this by continuing to ask the magical question we often asked as a three-year-old of our parents: why? The great management theorist Edward Deming, the originator of the quality movement in business, discussed this as the power of asking *why* five times to get to the root cause of the problem one is experiencing. The insight is the identification of the core issues driving the behaviors. For the Toby case, he would have come to the insight that he was feeling things that were familiar patterns for him from his core wounds as a child, namely being overly controlled and thereby wanting independence. The result would be to realize the overall dynamic at play and intervene proactively as described previously instead of acting out the usual patterns. Gaining insight into your belief window or system and the origin of that belief and the subsequent impact on habits and ineffective behaviors is the goal of this step in the process. Only after that can we come up with a meaningful solution that is not a Band-Aid approach addressing only symptoms and not the root cause of the pattern.

The variable CA represents a coherent plan of action. The plan would be a combination of the short-term inner technology solutions I described previously and longer-term solutions like the cultivation of the mind and perhaps more intensive exploration of family of origin patterns and resulting feelings and behavior patterns. In any case, the plan would include actions you can commit to and are motivated to try, as well as skills described in chapters 6 and 7 that would equip you for the journey. You can customize your plan by pulling from the resources described in the book so far.

There are two important elements that should be included in your plan of action. The first is involving others in your plan to support you and to help to hold you accountable. The second is holding yourself accountable. This could be as simple as a goal sheet with a scorecard of successes in the target areas you are seeking to change. It could also be a weekly meeting with one or two of your key support team to check in to see how things are going, receive support, and brainstorm methods to continue to grow and improve.

There is much research that indicates that writing down a plan with goals, actions, and measures of success is a powerful agent of lasting change. Without this, we do not have a large enough anchor to keep us stable, focused, and in the game of change.

The AAR variable is an after-action review. In this case, it means that when feelings start to lessen, when you are out of the white water of the stress and anxiety of the moment, when you are more resilient and resourced, take time to study what happened and why. Study also what your response patterns look like and how they are both ineffective and are often repeated without much thought involved. This review will sharpen your self-awareness skills to be able to catch the dynamic earlier and intervene earlier and more completely to get ahead of the curve the next time you are hijacked by an old feeling.

Applying this formula for a linear thinking person amounts to plugging in the values for each variable. The value increases in an additive fashion as we add greater insight to the actions we take and the understanding we have about the situation. It assumes that we have learned how to do the things outlined in the formula well and have a commitment to their development in ourselves. Like the old Pac-Man game, you would gain greater strength with each piece of the solution equation you select and apply. The more the better, and it is also true that any single choice applied well would get you started and build confidence and slow down your mind. Learning and building skills is the most important thing in this process.

THE JOURNEYMAN HUMAN SYSTEM DESIGN MODEL

The third and final tool to support your journey to positive lasting change is a framework I call the human system design model. (See Figure 8.1.) The process leads you step-by-step to assess your situation, set goals, and follow-through to achieve lasting change. Using this model will ensure that you are looking at your situation completely. I call this looking at the problem in a holistic manner. The value of doing this is that you go well beyond focusing only on the symptoms and look at the root cause of the problem you are facing. It also ensures that your plan is considering a solution that is complete and well thought through. Your chances of lasting change increase exponentially when you approach both the diagnosis, the plan of action, and the follow-through in this manner. I will walk you through the key points of how to use it and, in the process, share some examples from my own life and also from the Toby case study.

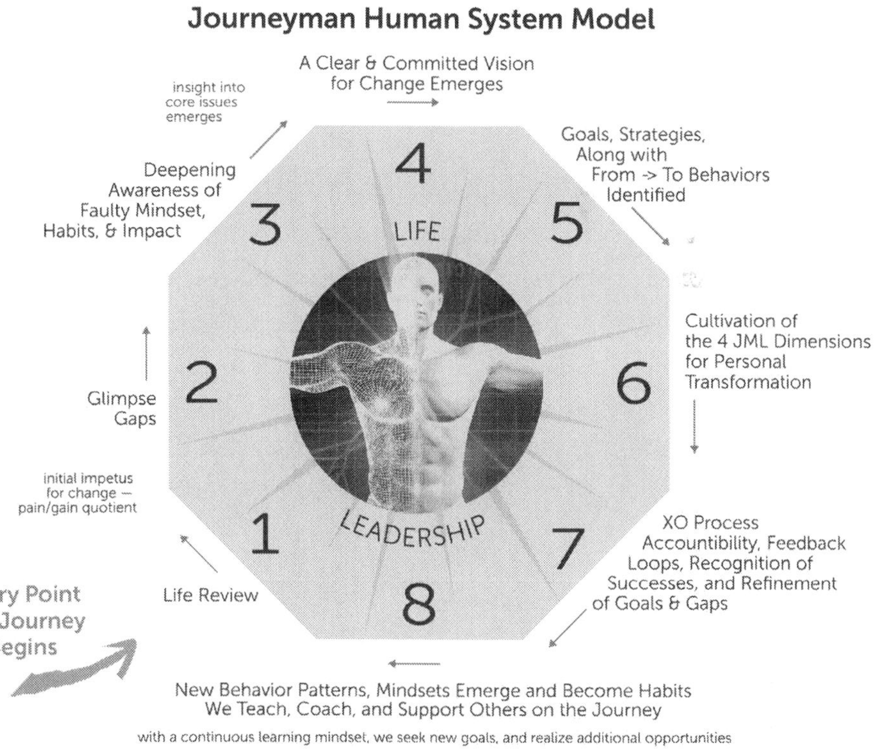

Journeyman Human System Model

A Clear & Committed Vision for Change Emerges

insight into core issues emerges

Deepening Awareness of Faulty Mindset, Habits, & Impact

Goals, Strategies, Along with From -> To Behaviors Identified

Cultivation of the 4 JML Dimensions for Personal Transformation

Glimpse Gaps

initial impetus for change — pain/gain quotient

Entry Point The Journey Begins

Life Review

XO Process Accountability, Feedback Loops, Recognition of Successes, and Refinement of Goals & Gaps

LIFE

LEADERSHIP

New Behavior Patterns, Mindsets Emerge and Become Habits
We Teach, Coach, and Support Others on the Journey
with a continuous learning mindset, we seek new goals, and realize additional opportunities

Figure 8.1

We can call this a life leadership model as it represents a cycle or map of how you can examine your life and lead yourself proactively to a better place.

Step 1: Life review

We usually enter the model at the seven o'clock position on the circle where it says Step 1, Life Review. There is some data point, feeling, or challenge that you are experiencing that is not going well from either your perspective or from the perspective of someone important in your life. At age thirty-eight, Toby's inner life was dominated by challenging negative thoughts and feelings about his life. He began experiencing depression and even behaving differently. Those were signs or symptoms of some other set of dynamics kicking in and overloading the system. These usually signal the impetus for change as the balance of life is off tilt. You will also note in small letters near this the idea that it signals the pain/gain motivation to think about change. We change either because we are in pain or fear, or we are doing well and have a lofty vision we want to achieve. Either of these can be sufficient to bring you to the doorstep of change and give you the will to go through the seven remaining steps in the journey. You may be interested in a simple and straightforward life assessment using this model. If so, please follow the link to access this survey at www.thejourneymanlife.com

Step 2: Glimpse gaps

This step is designed to provide an initial impetus and curiosity to kickstart the change process. The concept of a "glimpse" and how it can be a significant accelerant in change came to me while watching

The Family Man, one of my favorite movies. In the movie, Nicolas Cage gets a glimpse of how different his life could be in an alternate future with a few tweaks. The glimpse causes him to better appreciate his life and to double down on his commitment to his wife, his work, and finding more of a sense of purpose. This step, the glimpse, is a bit like that in that it is based on a snapshot assessment of your life. In a sense, it's like a peek behind the curtain to see if there's enough of a gap or impetus to move you into the next step of the process. Ultimately resolving the gap becomes the motivating factor for focus and a sense of urgency in driving a person to become totally committed to the process of change in going through the remainder of the steps in the process.

Step 3: Deepening awareness

This is a critical step in the change process. It is in a sense the make-or-break piece of the equation. The desire, the intent, the awareness, and the willingness to question yourself and take responsibility for your behaviors and the impacts they are having in your life is both uncommon and a massive differentiator between success and failure in this process. It involves a deeper review and accounting of who you have become, the habits and behavior patterns, the skills in communication and decision-making you have refined or not.

Toby feeling he was going off the rails at age thirty-eight could have kickstarted this process of deepening awareness. Instead, he took the path of least resistance and acted out his feelings, succumbing to his ego and lesser self. If he was aware of the opportunity that taking this step would have yielded him, his time travel map would have landed him in a different location and changed his life trajectory.

Step 4: A clear and committed vision

At some point in step 3, you think about the gap you have identified, and you start to wonder what your vision of this behavior change might look like if you were operating at the highest level in your life and what the resultant impact would be on your life success and well-being overall. You visualize it, perhaps journal about it, and it becomes a thing in your mind's eye and heart. An exercise that could be useful here is called *Remembering the Future*. In this visualization, you imagine that it is, say, five years out from today, and you have developed the new skills and mindset you have identified in your gap/glimpse. That is the desired future. Then you ask yourself how you accomplished that change. What steps did you take? How does it feel to be in that place? The more that you can feel into the future self/state, the more motivation you will generate to move toward that vision.

Step 5: Goals and from–to behaviors

One magical move to make in change is to identify the behaviors you want to move away from and the ones you want to move toward in your improved life. For Toby in our case study, he wanted to move away from the feelings of isolation, longing for something else in life, and frustration with his current situation, and move toward acceptance, love, understanding, and gratitude for what he did have. He wanted to move toward being aligned in his values and behaviors and away from the discontinuity that he felt inside himself. We have already discussed the power then of matching goals and strategies to accomplish those goals to the desired future state you seek.

Step 6: Cultivating of the inner and outer skills

In chapters 6 and 7, we looked at the skills needed to be successful on the journey. This mental and psychological conditioning and refinement is critical to actualize the goals set in step 5. You might select one or two at a time to develop. You might recall the information we discussed on learning styles and approach earlier in the book to help in this pursuit. Toby might have selected meditation, quieting his mind, slowing his mind down to access intuition and his inner sage voices instead of being at the mercy of the voices of his reactive mind.

Step 7: Accountability to yourself

Everything you have done up to this point in the journey process is critical, and without this step's ask, goes by the wayside. There are a few things that we have suggested to ensure success in this area. One is building and engaging a success network or board of directors to support you in the changes you have outlined. The other is to have a scoreboard with the lag measures for success, the actual impacts of difference you and others will see, and the lead measure or the actions you must take each day and each week to move you closer step-by-step to your goal.

Step 8: New patterns emerge

We notice and track our smallest successes in our mind, heart, and actual behaviors in the moments of truth and overall habits. We share our success with others, stay focused, and keep doing the things we have been doing so we do not fall off the wagon, as they say in AA. We also teach, coach, lead, and model the things we have lived with others to be a better leader in the communities where we live. We will discuss what this looks like in chapter 10 of this book. We realize that each day, each week we must keep on the journey and continue doing the things that have helped us.

We complete the 8 steps of the human design model for change, and we are back at step 1 again where we continue to diagnose, view the next mountain top, and set our sights on it from this new place. We realize that we are better equipped now to ascend to a higher peak because of the skills and experience we have gained, and we are grateful for that.

We also realize that the destination we seek is not a place where we will arrive and stay. We realize that the process is ongoing; the journey is constant, and the fruit of that journey is our well-being and that of others in our lives because we are living in this manner.

CHAPTER 9

WHAT'S AT STAKE FOR YOU, THE JOURNEYMAN?

W
hen I ponder the most important things in my life, most everything else except for my relationship with Teresa would take a distant second to the love that I have for my two adult children. That is more understandable when I pause and consider how much of my life has been invested in the care, nurturing, and love of them when they were infants, toddlers, teens, and now as adults; I can see why that is true. But as you likely know, it is more than those logistical and nurturing events that bind us to our children. We would do most anything for them. While this is the case for my dear daughter and son, it is also true for my grandchildren as well. I have four now, and I am amazed at how much I love, revere, and relive life through their vantage point and the eyes of their amazing parents. My son, Timo, has two almost-teenage girls, Ryan and Julia, and my daughter, Morgan, has three-year-old Addie and one-year-old James. (I am going to call him Jamesy, because I

like this name, and his parents have hinted that they might use that as his nickname.)

The above factors and many other things are the high stakes at play for the journeyman that will provide important altruistic and personal motivation for the journey. What is at stake for me is best evaluated through the lens of these four incredible grandkids of mine. I want to be a role model for them, and of course, I also want them to see and remember me as a guide who lived a value-based life and took his personal journey very seriously. I want to be the very best version of myself I can be.

There is also a more altruistic element to what is at stake for the world that they will live in when they grow to be adults. The many challenging aspects to modern life are piling up, brimming over, and landing squarely on our children. The role and effectiveness of the masculine archetype is one of those critical pieces of the puzzle of the future for our kids.

For example, my journey will likely influence Jamesy and his future life. Let's consider what his life as a man might look like if he were to see the world as we have discussed it so far. Jamesy is just starting to walk, talk, and develop his personality. Like all grandkids, he is an incredible boy! He is smiling all the time, engaged, happy, loving, and learning new things every hour of his young life. I love him very much and hope to be in his life as he grows up. I hope that he becomes an awakened man, one who is taking on and conquering emotional, personal, and spiritual growth opportunities in his life. I hope that he is the kind of man who takes responsibility for his life and his actions, that he is thoughtful, loving, kind, and trust-worthy. I hope that he sees that all people of the world, regardless of their ethnic, social, or religious background, are beautiful and deserve his respect. I hope his life has a balance of masculine and feminine energies, that he is sensitive and strong, brave and empathic, under-standing and decisive, supportive and thoughtful. I hope he feels his feelings, shares them with his loved ones and with others he trusts. I hope he has a rich inner life and that he cultivates his inner skills and values. I hope that he will take his personal development seriously, working on himself, equipping himself with the skills to travel on the journey of a man's life in a conscious and loving manner. I hope he learns about the moments of truth in his life and can slow his mind to be able to consider thoughtful and value-based responses to the most challenging situations.

I am sure that each of you reading this book has a similar vision of hope for the person your grandchild might become. The more important question is whether you have a plan to accompany that vision. How is it that he will not experience similar trauma, dynamics, events in and outside of his family that will shape his life experience as a man? What are the chances that he will live in a family, commu-nity, and society that will hold this emerging and more kind, aware, and skillful masculine mode?

The hope that I have for Jamesy is the hope I have for all young boys, young adult men, men in their mid-life, and even men in the latter stages of their journey to a well-lived life. That is what is at stake for us and for our world.

Shifting Masculinity

When I was considering the design of this chapter, I originally thought I would write about the emergence of a modern version of men and masculinity in our society, one where the concept of the alpha male is less prevalent, where the *anima*, as psychologist Carl Jung called the unconscious feminine side of a man, was more visible and accepted.

I was hoping for a world where I would write about how young men were no longer "losing their smile," as described in the *Book of Man*. I long for an emerging consciousness, where the ideal of manliness is not the cult ideal of super strength outlined by the Good Man Project.

All of these important sociological and psychological shifts are in process along with other gender-neutral sensitivities and norms that are proving to shift our view of sexual differences and preferences to be more inclusive and respectful. While we are not there yet by a long shot, momentum is building in that direction, and there is a plethora of great thinking, writing, and podcasts in this area. More and more, the immature behaviors of grown men in powerful positions are brought before us in news stories about how men make bad decisions that forever compromise their lives and the lives of their loved ones. It has become very clear that money, success, and power do not equal value-based, principle-centered actions.

In fact, one might even make the case that this type of privilege even promotes negative behaviors. Even with this landscape and landslide of misgivings among men, they are still in positions of power, and they continue to abuse their roles and privileges and even double down on their lies and bad decisions as having merit.

Thankfully, women are moving into leadership positions in all sectors of our society, from government to big business and science, and their ability to have a balanced perspective of the feminine and masculine energies is tantamount. I hope that you will open yourself up to these important ideas and ways of thinking about men and masculinity. The stakes are very high for society and the world. Your potential transformation and growth are not only going to benefit you but also your family, your significant relationships, and other men, because you will become a role model. Your change holds exponential potential for our future well-being.

Zooming In and Out

As important as our consideration of the emerging role of the masculine model for our society and for the world, changing ourselves might be the most powerful action we could take for ourselves, our families, and even our society. This is a change that is totally in your control, that would benefit you and your loved ones, and that would ultimately serve to change the world. That is what is at stake for us!

Imagine having the ability to zoom in on details we want to see in our lives and to zoom out to see the big perspective and how things fit together, like a Google Maps of your life. We have discussed how you personally can move toward your vision of a well-lived life.

Initially, I asked you to zoom in very closely to your own home base, to examine the inner reaches of your outer space, as Joseph Campbell suggested. We did so by analyzing the impact of that inner game on how you are living your values and vision. The first impact is on you, your beliefs, your behaviors, your habits, as a man, a role model in your life—your own self-respect, happiness, health, and well-being. You are the vessel that brings possible change into the world and keeping that vessel healthy and finely tuned is the most important job you have in changing the world.

Then we might zoom out to observe the impact of our beliefs and behaviors on our significant other and see what is at stake in that relationship. It's a bit like in the Dickens classic, when the character Scrooge, while visited in the dark night of his soul, was able to see the lives of the Cratchit family in a more empathic manner to change his perspective. We could then zoom out farther again and observe the impact of our behavior as a man as it relates to our family, our beloved children, daughters, and sons who look up to us for guidance and direction. We move the zoom lens even farther and see the impact on our professional associates, and we examine our leadership.

We can zoom farther out to see the impact of our habits and role as a man on our communities, our friends, our church, our volunteer life, our sport teams, and even consider what is at stake as a steward of our country and our democracy. We zoom even more distantly to see how we can impact our planet as she faces the dramatic impacts of global warming and world destruction through wars and other inconsiderate behaviors. Lastly, we zoom to the farthest realms of the universe to view our spiritual life to see the impact of our positive masculinity on the meaning and purpose of life itself.

To gauge the potential impact of moving from the historical past and current model of the masculine to a model of positive masculinity, which embodies both the yin and yang energies of life force itself, let us take a closer look at the behaviors and mindsets associated with each and the resulting impact on the key stakeholders of our life in each of the zoom levels identified above. This will give us the most poignant view of what actually is at stake for you.

It would be hard to argue with the fact that vast changes in technology, health, science, information availability, and the hard side of communications have taken place at the speed of sound in the past twenty years. It wouldn't be as hard to argue about the impact that those changes have had in our quality of life as we are still adapting to new ways of living with that technology and the associated trade-offs we make. What would be very difficult to argue with is the fact that we have made very little progress; in fact, we might even have slipped backwards a bit with respect to the relational side of life, including communication, empathy, respect for others, and compassion for our fellow person and planet. If the former represents the hard side of change, the latter we can call the softer side of change. Included in that aspect of our lives is also the notion of living in a state of integrity with our own values and proven principles of effectiveness. As our world becomes more complex, this too has become more difficult to navigate and takes tremendous focus to achieve.

It is also true that, in fact, it is because of changes like artificial intelligence, health advances, military weaponry, pandemics, and the inequality of wealth in the world that we are faced with more existential threats in our lives than ever before. I am very fearful of the world that Jamesy will likely find his host forty years from now as he builds his family and career. The stakes are high for all of us because of this change, and our fate rests on the decisions and actions of leaders who might be compromised in their relating and decision-making.

I have pondered the growing importance of emotional intelligence, win–win thinking, and a growing maturing of the inner side of our lives becoming even more critical to success in business, families, and overall life in these advanced technological scenarios. Technology will serve to even the playing field for business as what was once a differentiator will now become a commodity. What will separate the average from the superior performers will likely be the ability that the leaders in business will develop to make decisions, evaluate options, work in partnership with others, and be ethical in that process. In other words, the emotional, more personal, relational, and strategic side of leadership and change will come to matter more in our lives in the future. The same is likely true for family and community as the speed of change presents so many options and choices that we will need to be anchored in our family values to be able to raise our children and live in community in a conscious manner.

The net of all of this is that our personal journey will become more critical and have more of a stake in our success and happiness and well-being in the future than it has up to now, because it will be a lonely and critical anchor in the ever-increasing white water of our future lives.

With all of that as a backdrop to the stakes for our journey, let's go back to our mental Google Map and see what is possible with the growing importance of this softer side of our living. Let us see the impact of our becoming world class in refining and understanding our internal lives and our relationship with others. You can decide for yourself if the case for change that the journeyman vision postulates is likely to produce the pivotal positive impact to drive the changes necessary to address what is at stake for us personally, for our society, and for the world.

The Traditional Model of Masculinity

We have explored the behavior set, beliefs, and tendencies that have driven the prevailing model of the masculine over the past century. The twelve behavior tendencies outlined next emerge out of the vast amount of research in this area. They are tendencies that are evident in the more toxic model of masculinity. Each and every one of them has a negative effect on outcomes long term, and we have a stake in changing this model. This is the behavior set we are trying to move away from in our journey to a well-lived life.

These are in no particular order of importance:

- Being overly focused on control and always being in control of situations, decisions, and communication in relationships and relating to others

- A driving motivation to succeed, often without concern for others

- Being the alpha male, dominant and strong no matter the consequence

- Maintaining distance from others, approaching life independently; possibly being aloof

- Preserving one's image and persona as strong, successful, and in control

- Judging others or putting others down to keep oneself one-up at all times

- Being protective of oneself at all times

- Being of a singular focus in one's life without regard for others

- Not being in touch with one's own feelings, and certainly not expressing them to others

- Allowing addictions that perpetuate the numbing of feelings to eventually take over one's life at great cost to others, including loved ones

- Likely to be aggressive and angry in situations that test one's ego and image; acting out to show strength

- Mental and/or physical disorder appears in response to stuffing feelings and introverted anxiety and anger due to overwork, overstress, and not taking care of one's emotional or physical health

If you consider what it is generally like to live with, work with, parent with, or be in a significant other relationship with this prototype of a man, you can easily see/extrapolate the impact on others, decisions, planning, and relating. If you recall our earlier discussion, nearly 70 percent of men are testing in a reactive mindset and lack mature beliefs and behaviors. The vast majority of men have this profile. The net result is that decisions and actions that business, government, communities, and families make are coming from a faulty paradigm of toxic masculinity. That is what is at stake if we do not evolve this model of men and you do not pursue the change vision and goals you have made inside and outside of yourself.

The Emergent Model of Masculinity

The following behaviors, beliefs, and skills have a strong correlation to effectiveness, happiness, well-being, and overall positive outcomes in business, relationships, family matters, and community work that you pursue as male leaders in our world. These elements will guide us as we consider our changes and what is at stake for the key stakeholders and the impact on our lives. Once again, they are not in order of importance as each one is critical

THE DRIVE TO LEARN

There is a drive to be a learner in life, to be open to change, open to feedback, open to the thoughts and feelings and experiences of others. He can see beyond himself and his ideas. He is willing and excited about diverging from his point of view to open himself to new possibilities.

AWARENESS OF INNER DYNAMICS

He is aware of his inner dynamics, the voices of the reactive mindset that have been ingrained in him over the years. He works hard to tame those voices in himself. He is in touch with his feelings, knows them, lets them flow, and does not react to others based on his feelings. He knows how to take time and get centered to take whatever

WHAT'S AT STAKE FOR YOU, THE JOURNEYMAN?

information he needs from those feelings and make rational decisions based on his values.

A WILLINGNESS TO CULTIVATE THE MIND

There is a willingness to cultivate one's mind, to slow down the reactive thinking, in a sense to quell the ego and persona reactive voices inside us seeking to control our every response.

COMPASSION

In this model, men are more accepting, understanding, empathic, and compassionate for others and situations. This happens as we cultivate the skills for the journey outlined in the earlier chapters—specifically, the skills of dialogue and deep listening.

OPENNESS TO PARTNERSHIPS

In this framework for living, men are open to partnering with others, less focused on doing it alone, and more in concert with others to achieve a win-win outcome. To do so, men build trust with others through compassionate dialogue.

CULTIVATE PSYCHOLOGICAL SAFETY

In order to bring out the best in others, men move away from dominating and toward cultivating psychological safety with people. Research has shown time and again how critical this is for people to contribute their best and to be creative and transparent in their feelings and thoughts.

DEFINED VALUES

Men dig deeply inside themselves to discover and define the values and principles that they aspire to live by, that represent the best version of themselves. This rich inner work allows one to bring those values forth in the moments of truth when he would otherwise be guided by his reactive and less mature voices.

RESILIENCE

In this model of the masculine, the journeyman cultivates a healthy sense of resilience in his body and mind. This creates a grounded and peaceful yet strong energy that is valued by others. This balance in life becomes a model and strategy for others to strive for.

GRATITUDE

There is always a sense and feeling of gratitude for the graces given to him in his life. He is humble and thankful for all that he and his loved ones have in life and is considerate of those less fortunate. Positivity infuses his life as he focuses on the positives in situations and people.

COURAGE AND CONSIDERATION

In order to achieve positive long-term outcomes in life with others, he balances courage and consideration in his negotiations with others, even those who seem to have different beliefs and positions. He strives to find the third alternative that might be a creative and different solution, one that neither party had considered at first blush.

PEACE

The modern man has love and peace in his heart, not anger and a competitive nature.

LIGHTS ON

The smile that might have been quelled as a young boy early in life is present as those around him see and feel that the lights are on in his eyes and through his open arms.

Imagine that you are leading and interacting with loved ones and others in your world in this manner. Imagine the impact of these behaviors consistently applied across all situations. Imagine the impact on your sons and daughters, your significant other, your coworkers, your extended family. Imagine if you were in a significant leadership position and you had the opportunity to guide, teach, and be a role model to other men for these behaviors. What a great legacy that might be for you. What is at stake is not only getting right with yourself, but also getting right with others in your life. The opportunity is before you to become a role model, a transition person in your family of origin lineage to break the generational patterns of behavior that are insidious and habitual—habits and beliefs that drive behavior and thought, things that are so ingrained in us that we are hardly aware of their impact on ourselves and others. That is what is at stake.

The Journey to Becoming a Man for the Future

The bridge from this emergent model of masculinity to our next step on the journey is to zoom in and envision what it would take for my dear grandson Jamesy to develop into a man with a full embodiment of the emerging model of the masculine. One of the most important things you could and will do as a man to that end is to decide to work on your own improvement and awareness, but also to father your children in a manner that breaks that generational dynamic that created those behavioral tendencies in yourself. Likely, more than anything else in your life, those two actions or missions would provide the most value you could share in your life in the service of the new model of masculinity.

How many times have you heard the expression "a chip off the old block," referring usually to a man and his son? The *chip* that we are referring to is usually some notable and not-so-admirable trait that we seem to have inherited magically, when really what happened was that we learned it from our father. We even marvel at ourselves when at some point in our lives we realize that we are thinking, behaving, and acting just like our mother or father. That marveling is not so fun when we consider the bundle of negative, maladaptive actions and beliefs that we pass on to our kids. Blessings to you if you had a great role model in your parents and have found peace with whatever they did in their parenting that was not perfect. Becoming a conscious parent, stopping that negative transmission, and working on yourself to rid the baggage that has developed over the years is necessary to provide this opportunity for Jamesy and your children to live in a better world. One of the most exciting opportunities as a parent is to build a better model for your kids, your family. That is what is at stake and the heart of the matter.

There are a million ways that most parents likely unconsciously perpetuate the older societal norms of masculinity. First, let's discuss how that happens, then I will outline some ideas about how you can override those tendencies as parents of young boys.

For starters, research shows that there are important differences in the ways that parents treat boys and girls. Moms and dads both stressed achieving and being competitive with their sons. The parents in the study encouraged boys to always control their emotions, to be independent, and they were stricter in their discipline with boys. The parents often pushed for absolute conformity to external norm-based standards based on the traditional model of masculinity. Parents talked about their daughters using warmer and sensitive language and did more hugging with them than their male siblings. They also reinforced thoughtful introspection in their daughters, while at the same time holding a tighter hold on the girls than the boys as they were often rewarded for adventuresome actions. There are a host of other findings that researchers Jeanne Block and then Beverly Fagot noted that shed similar light on the differences in upbringing norms between boys and girls that substantiate the linkage to the traditional masculine model.

In his book *I Don't Want to Talk about It*, Dr. Terry Real reveals that the parents reported they were treating the sons and daughters exactly alike. This is one of the most shocking and informative conclusions from all this research. Systematically, parents were inadvertently stripping young boys of their feelings, sensitivities, and ultimately their ability to open their heart. Dr. Real goes on to state that little boys and girls start off with similar psychological profiles. They are more alike than different in terms of emotional, expressive responses and even physical affection. Over time, studies indicate that girls are permitted to remain expressive of their emotions with others, while boys are aggressively pushed out of this realm. He summarized this as the "loss of the relational" and credited it to three fundamental cut-offs for boys in early childhood: diminished connection to self, to others, and to the mother. This sets young boys up for the ensuing disassociation with their feelings and ultimately disconnection from themselves. This dynamic creates a fertile ground for the covert depression that frequently occurs in men.

These subtle and not-so-subtle messages are decoded by most boys as behavior required to be seen as manly. This dynamic is further reinforced by other boys and male adults who are their coaches and teachers, thereby substantiating the belief that this is the way they should behave to be seen as men.

In my case, in addition to my experience as a young boy and adolescent, I had other messages that exacerbated these tendencies. My mother was obsessed with achievement and getting ahead in life—beating out others, being better than others, and reveling in these results. It was not OK to lose, not OK to show weakness, not OK to be vulnerable. It was very clear to me what was expected, and that a man should push the limits of his abilities at all costs. Since I couldn't really rely on her because of her mental illness, I had to develop a fierce sense of independence. To make any of this work in my life, I had no choice but to stuff my feelings inside and to keep on taking her abuse and correction. As a result, I became isolated and withdrawn.

I was able to play the game of being manly. I was fortunate in that I was athletic and could compete in sports, but I never really felt whole in my life as the masculine model prevailed, and it was chipping away at my heart and soul bit by bit. The net result was that I was a persona, keeping up that façade and working hard to do so, but it was largely a house of cards that would come tumbling down later in life. That story is likely common to many young boys who become young men and then a man like Toby at age thirty-eight, a bit lost and not really having the foundation to understand his feelings and what to do about them other than act out and hold feelings in like he did his entire life.

A More Thoughtful Model of Raising Boys into Men

Many forces in society, including the environment, government, economy, health industry, educational challenges, urban and community planning, population issues, and certainly race and gender consciousness are converging in the decade of the 2020s, and the role and path of the masculine model are central to all that is at stake in those areas of our lives. Cultivating young men capable of becoming transition people and overcoming generational tendencies in the masculine becomes a key strategy in leading ourselves forward in dealing with these issues in a holistic, thoughtful, and conscious manner. In addition to this strategy, men are entirely capable in the later stages of our lives to turn around these stacked dynamics to become conscious men. But think of how exciting and powerful it would be to role model these behaviors with your own children and other young men and afford them a chance to build this authentic self from the ground floor up in their lives. Once again, that is what is at stake for the journeyman.

Just this morning, as I was outlining this chapter, I got a call from my daughter, Morgan, who lives outside Philadelphia, Pennsylvania. As I mentioned, Morgan and her husband, Graham, have two children: daughter Addie, age three, and son James, age one. As with most of our grown children these days, life during the year plus of the pandemic has been highly stressful with kids being at home and both parents working from home virtually in their extremely demanding careers; they have been tested in a multitude of ways as parents. It has been difficult to find time for meaningful connection during these months, and we all yearn for that. Morgan had a few minutes after dropping off the kids at daycare to check in with her dad. We have always been close and have had a loving, supportive relationship. She now has that with Graham, who is a thoughtful and loving father and husband, and I am thankful for that for her and the kids.

Morgan asked about the book I was writing, and I shared with her that in this chapter I was discussing how to raise a conscious boy in hopes that he would become a well-adjusted and balanced man. We discussed many of the issues that boys experience. The conversation shifted quickly to her thoughts about how she and Graham were studying as a part of a parent consciousness group to support—if not lead—their quest to be good parents and to hopefully, as she said, "break the generational patterns" of each of their families and the times that they were raised in. There have been and are many aspects to their parenting that I have noticed that are quite different than what I did with our son, Timo, and Morgan herself growing up. I am going to describe one of the approaches that is central to their parenting of both kids as it is aimed at perhaps the central issue at the core of the separation from self and feelings that men of my generation— and certainly I—have struggled with.

Teresa and I have noticed that when either of Morgan's children is upset for whatever reason, they take a totally different approach to addressing that upset. We also noticed on the other end of the spectrum that when either did something positive and noteworthy, they also take a different approach. Let me describe first the approach that I used as a parent—and likely you did as well—and we can take a look at the impact on some of the issues we have been discussing.

I described earlier the core or foundational universal dynamic for boys at age five is that moment or moments when he is told not to cry and not to express his sensitive feelings, and he learns to internalize those feelings instead. Morgan and Graham take the opposite approach; when Addie or James is frustrated, sad, or angry, they first acknowledge that they might be feeling something and even help them to identify the feeling: "You seem frustrated and even angry that your dad can't come down and play with you now. Is that what you are feeling? I can understand that is frustrating to you."

Notice what they did not do. They didn't try to snuff out the feeling, nor minimalize it, nor even try to make it OK for them. They did, however, witness the child's feelings and allow them to feel the feeling. They also encouraged them to discover how they could take care of themselves in that moment to address their frustration and feeling. An example of this is Morgan suggests to Addie that she has the opportunity to be alone and practice some breathing techniques they had taught her to cope with strong feelings and get a grip on herself. This approach strikes me as being very similar to the moments of truth interspace and the idea of invoking the four human endowments to find a better way to deal with feelings. Morgan pointed out the very thing that we have been highlighting in this chapter. She called it shifting generational patterns in family dynamics and ultimately setting the child up for greater success in life.

This is one simple yet profound example of a parenting approach that cultivates an entirely new set of behaviors in a child, behaviors that allow the child to stay connected with themselves and their feelings. Another huge impact of this process is that the child learns to rely on themselves to nurture and caretake in difficult situations and not expect another person to fix the situation and make it OK.

The opposite of this would be to minimize their feelings, making them wrong, modeling behaviors like control, power, and aggression that become a part of their behavior toolkit to use later in life. Each day in our relationships we deny or try to talk other people out of their feelings in an effort to interject our logic or feelings and ultimately control them. The by-product of this dialogue technique is similar to robbing your kids of their feelings.

Choose Your Path

We have explored the power of transformation and what is at stake for us, our families, our communities, and ultimately our planet. We have a choice as men on the path to face our patterning and behaviors to stand up to them. It is also true that when a man transforms his internal voices of the reactive mind, people see him differently, and he becomes a different person. When we resist less conscious behaviors that have evolved from historical traumatic events in our lives, we hold the opportunity to be a bridge from those generational masculine toxic tendencies to a place where kindness, consciousness, and ultimately greatness of heart prevail for ourselves, our loved ones, and the world.

There is much at stake, and every part of it lies inside you and your circle of influence. It is a choice you can make to transform yourself and, by example, our world.

CHAPTER 10

THE JOURNEY AHEAD

Across societies around the world in ancient times and modern, we humans have always been fascinated with the notion of an epic journey. What could be a better storyline than a great warrior, capable of deeds of great strength and courage, traveling over a vast setting encountering supernatural foes and prevailing with admirable humility. Men strive for greatness and to excel in so many aspects of their lives, and for many, that quest, that possibility, that challenge to be the best one can be and test the limits of human capability is what feeds their life.

While those endeavors in nature, as a working professional, in sport, in the military, are sexy and give our ego and persona a boost, for many who make these journeys outside of themselves, there is an inner mind that must be addressed and cultivated to push through the challenges and barriers that are always in front of us in these quests. The journeyman life is such a quest. Although it is focused externally on the achievement of a life well lived—your aspiration, dreams, and vision—we have seen in this book that the bulk of the heavy lifting is an inside job, having to do with taming and focusing our minds, which creates a belief window to the world of our habits. That journey is ahead of you and me, and the choice of beginning that trek is ours to make!

National bestselling author Michael Singer, in his book *The Search for Truth,* suggested that there are four aspects of the human experience. The body is on the physical plane of existence. The conscious mind is on the mental plane of life; it houses the Freudian concepts of id, ego, and superego. The third aspect is the subconscious mind or memory, and the fourth is the higher self, which is pure conscious energy or the superconscious mind. In this book, we have focused mainly on the conscious mind, where we live our daily lives, process information, and make decisions. To achieve our highest good in our lives or to live what we have been referring to as a well-lived life, many people believe that we need to address the concept of the higher self.

Most religions of the world and millions of people on Earth study and believe that there in fact are three aspects of our everyday experiences: the physical, the psychic or mind experience, and the spiritual experience. The central idea of the most important religions of our world is that man must evolve from the lower aspects of being to attain higher states of meaning. If you studied the major religions over thousands of years, you would learn that the basic truths behind them are similar. This is not a coincidence; they are all based on fundamental principles of living. Every major religion has a story of epic proportions that is the model and aspiration for the journey that men and women must undertake to ascend to a higher plane in this life and into the next. Whether you believe in the tenets of these religions or not, the notion of striving for and achieving our best selves on this planet, in this life, lives strongly in each of us. That notion, that yearning, is, in essence, what this book has been about. The not-so-perfect path is that journey for us, and whether it is to attain a higher spiritual plane or to be more loving and compassionate in this life is not the central question. We are on the path. We seek the path as we strive to be our best selves.

Buddhism, one of the most important religions of the world, has such an epic story. The story is that of Siddhartha Gautama, who was later to be known as the Buddha. He lived in India around 563 BC. He was the son of a wealthy royal family and lived his early years and married life in a palace. As he grew older and became aware of the suffering in the world, he wondered how this could be. He could find no answers to this and other existential questions, and one night, the story goes, he left his family in search of the truth. His quest took him to many places in India, and he studied with the most important thinkers of his time, seeking the answers to his questions about life. After seven years, still having no answers, while meditating in Bodh Gaya, India, he attained enlightenment. He went forth throughout India, sharing his insights and his gospels, and the Buddhist religion was born and spread to millions throughout the world.

Whatever your religious orientation is—or, for that matter, even if you are agnostic—this story, in one form or another, is common to all of us and certainly to those of us reading this book, on our own quest for some form of truth in our lives.

As it is with most epic stories and journeys, other seekers and followers over time keep the story alive by continuing to evolve it and perpetuate its key messages. Writer Philip Kapleau, in his book *The Three Pillars of Zen*, wrote about one such attempt in classic Buddhist writings, the famous ox-herding story, published in the twelfth century AD by Zen master Kakuen Shien. The story had ten image panels, each depicting a stage on the journey of a man, likely emanating from the original Buddha story. Following are the ten stages of the journey. As you read about them, you will be easily able to adapt the panel to the steps in the journeyman process I outlined in chapter 8 and your own quest on this epic journey.

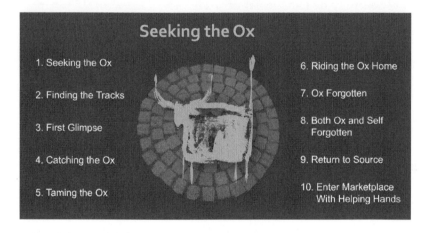

Seeking the Ox

1. Seeking the Ox

2. Finding the Tracks

3. First Glimpse

4. Catching the Ox

5. Taming the Ox

6. Riding the Ox Home

7. Ox Forgotten

8. Both Ox and Self Forgotten

9. Return to Source

10. Enter Marketplace With Helping Hands

Figure 10.1

The first panel is called "Seeking the Ox." Here, the man realizes that he is consumed by his lower self, and he feels a tug to ask, "Who am I? What is my purpose in life?" With this questioning, the epic search for the metaphorical ox—one's higher self—emerges as a quest. As with the journeyman process, we realize that we are going far astray and desire to course correct.

Panel 2 is called "Finding the Tracks." Here the man sees the writings on the wall of his life. He realizes that many have been in this place of challenge and questioning, and the tracks of those previous journeymen help him realize that there is a way out of this condition.

The third illustration is called "The First Glimpse of the Ox," and it is similar to the idea of seeing the gap in my life that I outlined in the journeyman process. The traveler must learn to concentrate deeply so that he can focus the proper energy within himself to see with clearer inner vision. This stage in the journeyman process is akin to the cultivation of the mind, or slowing the mind, to be ultimately able to perceive fundamental truths in life.

The fourth is called "Catching of the Ox." The man briefly sees his lower self in operation in the world; the importance of self-awareness is our takeaway. He realizes the ox is hard to tame and that he must be Zen-like to train the mind to ascend to a higher plane. It is interesting to note that Zen Buddhism is a branch that emphasizes not religious ritual and dogma but practices emphasizing focused and discipline in daily routines like meditation (*zazen*) to achieve higher states of man.

The fifth panel is called "Taming the Ox." Although it is difficult, the lower self—the senses, emotions, and desires—can be quelled and put in perspective. Untethered, the muddy haunts lead the ox astray as it willingly follows its master. This is likely where author Mickey Singer developed the notion that you can untie yourself from your ego, harness your inner strength, and reach for a better, more meaningful place in your life.

The sixth panel is "Riding the Ox Home." The struggle is ending. Our man sees his experience of either gain or loss with perspective. From the top of the ox's back, he gazes at the clouds above.

The seventh panel is "The Ox Forgotten, Self Alone." The Dharma (truth) is that we see the oneness in the world, the lack of duality, the man sits alone, and that is the truth of life.

The eighth stage of this epic journey is called "The Forgotten Self and Ox." This is the state of the "I am," the transcendence of the ego. The journeyman is at peace with himself. He ultimately realizes that he is all those things, inside and outside of himself, and begins to understand the expression "all is one."

The ninth illustration is "Returning to the Source." The journeyman returns to his origin, seated in his hut. He listens to the stream meandering through nature.

The last panel is called "Entering the Marketplace with Helping Hands." This is where the traveler enters back into daily life, equipped with fresh perspective and tools for the ongoing journey. He vows to help others on the path to undergo their own journey. This is the true test of success.

Several years ago, on an excursion in Florida, Teresa and I decided to take a short detour to Gainesville, Florida, to visit author Michael Singer at his thirty-year retreat center, where he has taught lessons concerning our journey toward the truths of the universe based on these teachings. He too had studied the work and teachings of someone who was a central person in my journey around age forty-five, Paramahansa Yogananda, who also wrote an epic book of his journey called *Autobiography of a Yogi*. I was amazed and delighted to see revered photos of Yogananda's face and his books at the center of Mickey Singer's alter, in front of which he delivered his daily *sanghas*.

Yogananda was a Hindu who came to America in the 1950s and established the Self-Realization Fellowship (SRF) in LA. He had an amazing following around the world to hear his teachings. The SRF still thrives in its retreat center in the hills of Southern California. I had the opportunity to visit the center and meditate with his direct disciples several years ago after I had completed a two-year guided study course on his practices under the guidance of the SRF. It was for me—and for Mickey Singer, as well—one of the most influential connections of my life, and it helped me to come to grips with how I could ride the ox home in my life. To this day, I still practice mediations, prayers, and lessons from this source.

Coming full circle, Singer's bestselling book *The Untethered Soul* is essentially about becoming free from limitations, soaring beyond your boundaries, finding inner peace and freedom, and learning to navigate your thoughts and emotions. Undoubtedly, Singer's work and the original work of Yogananda were an inspiration for this book and continue to be guiding me in my daily practices.

The Catalyst for My Journey

Men have always been attracted to the adventurous epic journey— the lure of the great challenge, the potential for greatness, and even the thrill of surviving great danger and overcoming incredible odds. As inviting as this is, in some ways, it is a distraction that allows us to keep the focus outside, on the exterior of our lives. The epic journey that may be the most challenging and most rewarding is the shortest journey of all time. It involves the fifteen centimeters that is the average span of the human brain from ear to ear. The stakes are high, the challenge is immense, and the reward is epic.

Indeed, the choice is yours—and only yours—to enter on this journey. I found myself faced with that choice a few years ago. Each of us, when we look back on our lives, has several memories that stand out above others among our multitude of experiences. One such memory for me became the impetus for me to commit to my own journey.

The story is about the passing of Big Tony, my father, and how his death opened up a part of me and propelled me in my choice to enter the journey in a more committed manner. I received a call from a thoughtful nurse at the home where we were forced to place him as his health deteriorated to the final stages of life. It was a Sunday afternoon in March. Big Tony had stage 4 lung cancer, and the cancer had spread throughout his body. He had been a career fireman, and the years of inhaling toxic smoke had likely caught up with him. Even so, when the diagnosis came, it was a shock to the family.

The cancer spread quickly, and the two months we had after that diagnosis were not enough to properly process his imminent death. In many ways, he didn't want to live any longer. He was not happy in his life for as long as I knew him, but when the end was near, I think it hit him hard, and he sobbed about his life and didn't want to have it end. On that Sunday, on that call, the nurse shared with me that his life force was slipping quickly and that I might want to be with him at the end. I so appreciated that call. I dropped everything and rushed to the nursing home in hopes that I could be with him in the end.

The home was about a twenty-minute drive away. When I got there, I found my dad close to his last breaths. He was a great guy. I loved him, but I had felt sorry for him my entire life, even as a child. There were about twenty other firefighters at the HQ station in our hometown of Waterbury, Connecticut, and I used to spend tons of time at the firehouse after school during my high school years. Everyone loved my dad. He was a kind, thoughtful, and fun person. He loved being with the guys at work and cherished the deep friendships and trust of the firefighter culture.

At home, things were different. He had a challenging marriage to my mom. Mother Mary was bigger than life itself and very difficult for him in so many ways. As I mentioned, she was diagnosed as an obsessive–compulsive neurotic, and she dominated him and their life in every way. He literally could not make a move without her consent, and he resented that greatly. For the most part, he stuffed those feelings down and likely experienced the covert depression we discussed earlier. He told me that he stayed in the marriage because of me and my sister, Dolores, suggesting that he didn't want to leave us alone with her. While I appreciated that sentiment, it was a life that was not well lived for Big Tony.

All of those feelings that I had inside me about the sadness of his life hardly ever escaped. Because of the immense guilt I felt about his life and the love I felt for him because of his inherent goodness, it was even more critical for me on that day, when he was close to death, to be with him. I wanted to support him as he had supported me, in his own way, throughout my life. Although we didn't hug much or at all and didn't share intimate moments, for some reason, without thinking much, my instincts propelled me to climb into the hospital bed with him and get behind him, his back at my chest, his head cradled in my hands, and my legs wrapped around him. I whispered softly in his ear that I loved him and thanked him for all he had done to keep my sister and me safe from the real peril my mom brought to our lives. Within several minutes, with my hand on his heart, I felt his last breath. I sobbed tears of sadness for his life. I had never been with anyone in that way at the end of their life, let alone my own dear father, and it was a profound experience.

That moment was a time of deep reflection for me. I had been thinking a great deal in my own life about what I wanted my life to be and the path I wanted to take spiritually and emotionally. I knew that I was challenged in many ways from growing up in this very dangerous and psychologically damaging home environment. I thought a great deal about the kind of person I wanted to be and what it might take for me to get to that point.

It all came to a head when preparing for delivering my dad's eulogy at his service at the church where we grew up, Our Lady of Mount Carmel, in the town plot section of Waterbury. What would I say about him? What would I say about life and death? In the silent moments of reflection over those several days, I realized that, for all my reading, study, degrees in psychology, meditation, and prayer, I still was stuck, much like he was in his life. I was stuck in my own past, in my trauma, and in the reactive tendencies that I had developed. I knew the path he had taken, and it didn't turn out well for him or for us. What path would I take? Would I learn from his story? Could I be a transition person in our family to break through the generational tendencies?

One thing I knew for sure that gave me some solace: Big Tony was a good person, and most everyone he knew thought of him as a good friend. Some people even called him a saint for putting up with my mom and giving away his life as he did to keep the family safe. In those days of deep reflection, I vowed to work on my life in the remaining years, to become a principled man, a courageous person, a person of dignity and authenticity, with the warmth and humility of my dad, to be both loving and honest about myself, my feelings, and my hopes and dreams.

This then became my epic journey, to dedicate myself to becoming the best version of myself that I could be in this life. What is the story or impetus for you to pull you over the line to consider changing some important elements of your life? What might motivate you to really take on this challenge? Is it a clear sense that you are heading down a path that is not what you would like for your life? Is it a strong vision that you have of how you would like to be living your life in the future? What is at stake for you, and where will you grab the motivation from to accelerate and sustain the energy needed? Is it for your children, your family, your professional goals, your purpose in life, your religious beliefs?

As we start to wind down this book and ramp up your own journey, it would be useful to consider those two questions. Let's look at the last few pieces of the puzzle.

Making a Choice and Sticking to It

Making a choice is a tricky business for humans, for sure. We often have lots of seemingly great ideas, goals, plans, and even commitments that do not come to fruition. In my professional practice as a consulting psychologist for over thirty years working with thousands of individuals, I have found that the majority of my clients have the ability, motivation, and skill to change, but only the most disciplined actually succeed.

To shed some light on those missing pieces, I want to introduce a final concept, tool, and framework that I learned about over twenty years ago that still is helping me most every day in making commitments and staying with them. Robert Fritz wrote a book in 1999 called *The Path of Least Resistance*. Fritz is an award-winning composer of music and a management and systems thinker. The central idea of the book is that the structure of our thinking is the biggest problem in approaching problems or goals. He distinguishes between two fundamental types of thinking, what he calls structural conflict and structural tension. The former leads to ineffective goal achievement, and the latter is central to success.

In the structural conflict paradigm, you are constantly vacillating between the pull of the goal and the fear that you can't achieve the goal or do the things necessary to make it come to fruition. Imagine yourself in a room with one wall representing the goal you have and the other the fears or challenges that you face in achieving that goal. To further illustrate the dynamic at play in this situation, imagine that there are two big elastic bands attached around your waist and each anchored to the respective walls. As you move toward your goal, you feel the pressure of the band attached to the fear wall, and it pulls you back to center or even more so toward the fear wall. As you move to the fear wall, you are reminded of the goal wall and how much you want and need to reach it. Your movement toward the fear wall again creates conflict and the pressure pulls you back to center or toward the goal wall. This dynamic creates an oscillating pattern that keeps you in a constant state of conflict. In a sense you are frozen in your tracks, and the result is little movement toward your goal.

I have found myself in this pattern of behavior over the years hundreds of times. How about you? It's disconcerting when you find yourself in this place, and it tends to freeze your ability to commit fully to the goal or plan. In a sense, you are not fully engaged or committed to the vision or goal; it's more like you are testing the waters. This does not work well in a situation where the stakes are this high, because a common psychological effect kicks in called the incorporation effect. We set a goal, incorporate the initial changes and learning, and then, when the pressure is on, we revert to our well-grooved patterns of behavior and become less committed to the change we had hoped for in our behavior. If, on the other hand, we can work through this incorporation stage of learning and keep our eyes on the prize, we have the opportunity to get to a new plateau in our results and learning. Hence the term incorporation effect. The question emerges: How do we get out of this oscillating pattern?

Fritz suggests that there are three basic choices we must make to escape this pattern. The first is called the fundamental choice. This is the choice and acceptance that we are the creative force in our lives, not a victim or someone who is reactive to circumstances outside of ourselves. This is very similar to the story I told earlier about Austrian psychiatrist Viktor Frankl, who was a Nazi concentration camp victim.

The second choice is called a primary choice, which defines your change vision and what you want to attain—your goal, the end you have in mind. The level of commitment in this choice is clear and strong. We do not concern ourselves with how it can be attained at this stage, as that can diminish our commitment to the goal in a pure sense. The metaphor that Fritz uses to describe this second structural thinking approach is that you see a cloud in the sky, your vision or goal. You put all your energy into the vision, clarity, feelings, emotions, and gratitude for achieving it, and then you imagine a string or rope attached to that cloud around your waist like the rubber band in the previous structural conflict model. The anchor is in you, your grounded understanding and assessment of your current reality.

While you hold and are honest about your reality, you systematically identify the third type of choice, which he calls secondary choices. These are smaller but not less important goals and learning that will systematically move you toward your vision and the cloud. Your commitment remains strong, and your resolve is intense.

It is sometimes difficult to be in this second structural thinking paradigm because we are in the whitewater of daily life and in reactive, stressful moments we can revert to the structural conflict model, just like what I described in the incorporation effect. I believe that Fritz called this the path of least resistance because we are eliminating the main interference inherent in the conflict model, which is our fear of the challenges the goal attainment creates.

When we think about our choice to enter into the path of the journeyman, it is with the resolve in the structural tension model that will be needed.

Where Do We Go from Here?

If you have made it this far, it is likely that you are experiencing either some discomfort or challenge in your life, or you are intrigued by the possibility of an upgrade in your life's operating system. For me, it was a bit of both that inspired me in the past and does so still today. The question that looms for you is this: What can you do—what actions can you take—to make the important first step on your journey?

I designed our conversation to provide two important things. One was to help give you perspective on your situation, a way to think about the challenges you are experiencing. The second was to provide a roadmap for you to follow in the journey process to achieve the goals that you aspire to in life. I would start with a realistic assessment of your situation, what is working for you and your loved ones and what is not working. Identifying that gap and getting a glimpse of a vision of a better you, a more fulfilled you, an openhearted and healthy you is the next step. Then would be to identify shorter-term goals, selecting and learning about the skills for the journey, and beginning to work on their development. The final element in the journey would be the identification of a support team and engaging them in your effort in a meaningful manner.

A great resource that you may find helpful to kickstart your journey is to consider accessing some of tools the Journeyman Organization will be providing. Soon after the publication of this book, we will be organizing eight-man training groups. The groups will provide training in the skills for the journey, support for the psychological aspects needed to succeed, and provide certification for the interested man to be able to lead groups of men in your community using the journeyman approach. In my experience as a university professor, business consultant, coach, and executive trainer, I have discovered that the best way to learn about these skills and to gain the motivation to sustain your journey is to teach others and to continue to be involved in teaching, coaching, and learning with and from others. What a wonderful win–win situation that would be as you deepen your learning and commitment to positive change and also help other men along this journey. If you are interested in this, please contact me through our website at www.thejourneymanlife.com.

Where Am I on the Journey Today

Approximately ten years ago, while visiting our family in the Boulder, Colorado, area, I heard about a spiritual teacher and intuitive by the name of Robert Wood. My sister-in-law, Barb Edwards, shared with me the great value she had experienced in a consultation session with Bobby, and that he had a unique approach to "reading" a person and tapping into the realms of the superconscious where individuals with a predisposition and dedicated practice can access those realms of life for clients who are open to listening and learning.

On my own path to improving myself, I have certainly read, listened to, and studied with a wide variety of sage thinkers in the field of human development, psychology, experiential education, and spiritual thinking. I have come to believe that there is much I do not know about how the universe works. There are forces and energies operating around us that are unknowable but available if we open our hearts, minds, and souls to their messages and gifts. While I believe this, I also see myself—and I think if you asked, most people would see me—as a very grounded and realistic person. My experience with Bobby Wood pushes the boundaries of that grounded reality orientation.

I went to Bobby's office home, several miles up a canyon road outside of Boulder. As Bobby invited me into his home, I couldn't help but notice the hundreds of stones that were around. I found him a jovial and kind person, very unassuming and comfortable to be with. I must admit that I continued to be a bit anxious about what was going to happen in the reading. He had cultivated a method of reading energy and accessing spirit guides through the rocks in his room. He asked me to select several rocks that I was drawn to, and he put them in front of us and began sharing thoughts about my life.

Each thing he shared was spine-tinglingly accurate and tremendously meaningful to me. He had captured my deepest attention and trust within twenty minutes. After he had shared for a while, he asked me what questions I had for the spirit guides about my life. I asked him about the journey that I had been on, what the meaning and purpose of the challenges I had growing up were about, and where I was in my life journey now and might be in the future. What he shared with me next resonated to the core with my own intuition and knowing about my life. It was so accurate and to the point that only I could know or conceive of it.

He said that the spirit guides acknowledged the growth I had made in my life in overcoming the challenges and living successfully. He said that they felt I could feel good about the progress my soul had made in this life. I remember feeling so acknowledged and very proud and grateful for what I was able to do in my life up to that time with the challenges that I had lived through in childhood and into my twenties and beyond. It was a bit of a relief because I had tried very hard to overcome the demons inside me, but I knew the fight was constant and unending.

I suppose that I could have ended the session there and declared victory for this session and my life at that point, but he asked if there was anything else. There was something else that I knew was festering inside me, a regular point of conversation with Teresa, who is a constant and wise seeker of the truth in life and conscious living. I asked him what else was left for me to do in this lifetime. His answer still resonates so deeply in me to this day. This is what he said: There was another stage in my soul's evolution on Earth that was available to me if I was willing to open myself up to the challenge of looking deeper than ever at my inner life journey.

We ended our session, and as I exited his home, I knew that I had experienced something very profound and sacred. That idea, challenge, and opportunity has stayed top of mind the past ten years, since that day outside Boulder. It set up a constant reflection in my inner life, where I so often considered the implications of either moving toward Bobby's suggestion of my soul's journey or not doing the work necessary to advance in my life purpose.

What I experienced reminded me of the structural conflict story we discussed earlier. Metaphorically, I was in the room with the two walls, one being my current life and what I had accomplished so far, the other being a vision of another stage of my soul's journey taking me to a place of greater love, joy, understanding, and compassion with the world. The elastic bands were tugging me toward the vision and then pulling me back toward Fritz's path of least resistance.

I was in that state for many years, and then life presented a change for me that set me on the path to advance. I developed not one but two cancer diagnoses. The treatments to help heal the illness took me out of my current life and work for several years, and that reset helped me to decide that deeper reflection and action was indeed the course I wanted to take. Whether Bobby Wood was indeed tapping into a realm of existence beyond our knowledge and gaining this message from spirit guides or whether he saw something that indeed was in me, in my energy field, that clicked in him matters less to me now. What is true is that that session, that conversation, gave me a sign and information that this path, this journey to a life well lived, was indeed available to me in my future. I made a choice to take that path.

The impetus to dig deeper, to learn, to practice, to teach others came out of that story. The motivation to research and write this book about the practices and beliefs that are related to changing my life—and yours—came in that session. Now that I have written this book about my journey so far and the potential journey of my soul's future, I have but one thing to do, and that is to follow the path, to teach other men who are on that journey as well. I am in that place now, I am on the journey, striving to practice and become the things that you have read in this book, and I sincerely hope you come along on that journey with me.

Conclusion

The transformation process is difficult—as difficult as life itself. Our quest for the evolution of our own life is at stake, but in truth, the stakes are much higher than that. We risk the psychological, spiritual, and social imperative to evolve and mature the masculine psyche.

Joseph Campbell, in his last book, *The Inner Reaches of Outer Space,* beckons us to join this worldwide awakening. Robert Moore and Doug Gillette put it elegantly in the conclusion of their epic book, *Rediscovering the Archetypes of the Mature Masculine Psyche,* when they wrote that this "initiation of men would become a rallying point for a deepened human sense of responsibility and maturity." This is the outer reaches of the inner space that Campbell described.

I wish to add my voice—and, hopefully, you will add yours—to the many men throughout history who, against enormous odds, have called for an end to the reign of the less conscious, less responsible version of men in our society. We call for men to take on the task to own their initiation from boyhood to manhood, in the truest sense of the word, so that we might witness a new beginning instead of the beginning of the end.

Whether it be your personal journey, mine, or ours as men, the path has been cleared, and the choice is yours to make. The infinite power of commitment is captured in one of my favorite quotes from Scottish mountaineer William H. Murray: "Until one is committed, there is hesitancy, the chance to draw back, always ineffectiveness, concerning all acts of creation. There is one elementary truth, the ignorance of which kills countless ideas and splendid plans: that the moment one definitely commits oneself, then providence moves too." Join me in that commitment.

ACKNOWLEDGMENTS

The journey of life is indeed a personal experience with countless hours consumed by reflection on thoughts, experiences, ideas, and decisions. We come into the world alone and we leave alone. Even as that is true, the quality of our life, the richness, the depth of experience is truly a social experience with so many people contributing to who we are and who we have become. I have revered my individual strength, motivation, and striving for a life well lived, yet I know that I am who I am as a result of the relationships, the teachers, the roles, and multitude of rich experiences I have had in my life.

Following are some of the people who have been my closest friends and teachers, those who have lived with me, loved me, and urged me on in my life.

To my amazing wife Teresa for her incredible ability to love me! But she is much more than that to me. She has been a teacher of how to live life, how to strive for peace, love, and goodness. She is teaching me about compassion, empathy, friendship, and, most importantly, how to be the best version of myself and how to truly love another person.

I am so grateful for my two children, Timothy and Morgan, for the great relationship that we have had in our lives. We have learned how to love each other well. I am so proud of both of you for the amazing people you have become as parents, spouses, and professionals, and so grateful to your spouses, Jennifer and Graham, who are great partners to you and have always been uber-supportive of me as well.

I have had countless professional colleagues, both partners and clients, who have taught me, pushed me, supported me, but most of all have shown love to me. All my partners at Charter Oak Consulting Group—John, Neil, Cathy, Diane, Barry, Jim, Roberta, and others—have been dear friends and partners, and I owe each of you so much for who I am as a professional.

There are way too many others to name, but I know as you read this, you will know who you are!

I would like to single out two professional colleagues who were with me to birth my philosophy and practices in the field of organization psychology. Jonathan Spiegel, my partner and dear friend early on in our consulting adventure, taught me most of what I know about the field, and we were sidekicks through some amazing client adventures. The other, my business partner and great friend Kendall Lyman, has worked by my side with clients as we have grown our knowledge and practice in the field of organizational change, culminating in our book on that subject: *Change the Way You Change.* We've had countless learnings and countless laughs together.

To my dear friends in life who I talk with each day, have fun with, grow and learn from and with, I thank you for that. I hope that I can be a better friend over time. Much of my experience as a man has been through sport and competition, with golf and tennis being my great loves. I am eternally grateful for all my buddies who I walked the green grasses of the Washington Golf Club and the Ansley Golf Club over the years—walking alongside you for countless hours trying not to talk about the meaningful parts of life while in reality we were experiencing the most important part of life up close and personal. We were and are great friends and have explored so many parts of what it means to be human in those countless rounds of golf. Specifically, I would call out Matt, Richard, and David, who I have spent many hours of my life with over the years chasing the white ball!

To my dear extended family, and what an incredible family it is! My sister, Dolores, who was with me during our years as children together enduring the challenges of our family. My amazing sisters-in-law, Deb and Barbs, who are partner seekers in the world and beyond. My brothers-in-law, Rex, Chuck, Ian, and Ray, who I have had countless conversations with about our journey as men. Uncles and aunts have each and all contributed to what I have learned and continue to attempt to apply to make life better. To the late Barbara Bailey, my mother-in-law, who taught me through her inspirational life to wake up each day and "vote" to be a person who lives by their most precious values in life no matter what adversity the day might bring. We continue to grow and be on the journey together. I thank you Thyrza for our time together in the early parts of our lives as we both struggled to understand how we could live life, grow a family, and love ourselves and the other. I so appreciate our continued friendship and celebration of our family.

To my dear parents, Mary and Big Tony. You gave me so much love, and I learned much from your struggles but also from your life lessons and endless support. Your motivation to push me to continue my education was the greatest gift you could have given to me, along with your unending love.

I want to thank the team of professionals at Greenleaf Book Group for their incredible trust in me, their steadfast professionalism and support. What a great team to partner with on this book: Nathan, Jessica, Jay, Jen, and Daniel.

Lastly and perhaps most importantly, I want to thank my grandchildren, Ryan, Julia, Addie, and James. I love you so much and get so much love and energy in seeing you grow up and become the great people I know you will be in life. I owe you for my motivation and courage to write this book. When I originally conceived of it, at its most basic it was to pass a story along to you, a story of me and a story that might help you be the best person you can be in life based on my experience. I wanted to pass that along to the four of you. Each of you already shows me signs of your ability to love, be loved, be courageous, and stand for things that you believe. Your parents have been great teachers and role models for you. As you grow, I hope that the ideas and learnings from my life might benefit others growing up in your age group and thereby benefit the future of humanity and the well-being of our planet and all its creatures.

Thank you all!
The journey continues.

—Tony

BIBLIOGRAPHY

By Chapter

INTRODUCTION

Campbell, J. 1994. *Hero's Journey.* Random House Value Publishing.

Vaillant, George E.; Charles C. McArthur; and Arlie Bock, 2010, "Grant Study of Adult Development, 1938-2000," https://doi.org/10.7910/DVN/48WRX9, Harvard Dataverse, V4, UNF:6:FfCNPD1m9jk950Aomsriyg== [fileUN).

Hendricks, Gay. 1990. *Conscious Loving: The Journey to Co-Commitment.* New York, NY: Bantam Doubleday Dell Publishing Group.

Santos, Laurie. 2018. "The Science of Well-Being." March. https://www.coursera.org/learn/the-science-of-well-being.

Kahneman, Daniel. 2012. *Thinking, Fast and Slow.* Harlow, England: Penguin Books.

Maslow, Abraham H. 2020. *A Theory of Human Motivation.* Hawthorne, CA: BN Publishing.

CHAPTER 1

Jung, C. G. 1969. *Collected Works of C.g. Jung, Volume 9 (Part 1): Archetypes and the Collective Unconscious.* Edited by Gerhard Adler and R. F. C. Hull. Princeton, NJ: Princeton University Press.

Kegan, Robert. 1982. *Evolving Self: Problem and Process in Human Development.* London, England: Harvard University Press.

Moore, Robert, and Douglas Gillette. 1991. *King, Warrior, Magician, Lover: Rediscovering the Archetypes of the Mature Masculine.* London, England: HarperSanFrancisco.

CHAPTER 2

Deutschman, Alan. 2007. *Change or Die: The Three Keys to Change at Work and in Life.* New York, NY: HarperCollins.

"How Your Nervous System Works & Changes." 2021. Hubermanlab.Com. January 4, 2021. https://hubermanlab.com/how-your-nervous-system-works-and-changes/.

Kolb, David A. 1983. *Experiential Learning: Experience as the Source of Learning and Development.* Upper Saddle River, NJ: Financial Times Prentice Hall.

Mezirow, Jack. 1991. *Transformative Dimensions of Adult Learning.* London, England: Jossey-Bass.

CHAPTER 3

Jung, C. G. 1969. *Collected Works of C.g. Jung, Volume 9 (Part 1): Archetypes and the Collective Unconscious.* Edited by Gerhard Adler and R. F. C. Hull. Princeton, NJ: Princeton University Press.

Gladwell, Malcolm. 2009. *Outliers: The Story of Success.* Harlow, England: Penguin Books.

CHAPTER 4

Stone, Hal, and Sidra Winkelman. 1985. *Voice Dialogue.* Marina del Rey, CA: DeVorss.

CHAPTER 5

Covey, Stephen R. 2013. *The 7 Habits of Highly Effective People.* 25th ed. London, England: Simon & Schuster.

Frankl, Viktor E. 2006. *Man's Search for Meaning.* 4th ed. Boston, MA: Beacon Press.

Hendricks, Gay. 2010. *Five Wishes: How Answering One Simple Question Can Make Your Dreams Come True.* Novato, CA: New World Library.

Real, Terrence. 1998. *I Don't Want to Talk About It.* Dublin, Ireland: Newleaf.

Reichheld, Frederick, and Thomas Teal. 1996. *Loyalty Effect: The Hidden Force behind Growth, Profits and Lasting Value.* Boston, MA: Harvard Business Review Press.

CHAPTER 6

Anderson, Robert J., and William A. Adams. 2015. *Mastering Leadership: An Integrated Framework for Breakthrough Performance and Extraordinary Business*

Results. Edited by Robert J. Anderson and William A. Adams. Nashville, TN: John Wiley & Sons.

Branden, Nathaniel. 1995. *Six Pillars of Self-Esteem*. New York, NY: Random House.

Dweck, Carol S. 2008. *Mindset*. New York, NY: Ballantine Books.

Goleman, Daniel. 2007. *Emotional Intelligence*. 10th ed. New York, NY: Bantam Books.

Livingston, J. Sterling. 2003. "Pygmalion in Management. 1969." *Harvard Business Review* 81 (1): 97–106.

Yogananda, Paramahansa. 2004. *Autobiography of a Yogi*. Los Angeles, CA: Self-Realization Fellowship.

CHAPTER 7

Brown, Brené. 2010. "The Power of Vulnerability." Ted.com. June 2010. https://www.ted.com/talks/brene_brown_the_power_of_vulnerability.

Duhigg, Charles. 2016. "What Google Learned from Its Quest to Build the Perfect Team." *The New York Times*, February 25, 2016. https://www.nytimes.com/2016/02/28/magazine/what-google-learned-from-its-quest-to-build-the-perfect-team.html.

Losada, Marcial, and Emily Heaphy. 2004. "The Role of Positivity and Connectivity in the Performance of Business Teams: A Nonlinear Dynamics Model." *The American Behavioral Scientist* 47 (6): 740–65.

CHAPTER 8

Edwards Deming, W. 1988. *Out of the Crisis*. 2nd ed. Cambridge, England: Cambridge University Press.

Ratner, Brett. 2000. *The Family Man*. USA: Universal Pictures.

CHAPTER 9

Campbell, Joseph. 2012. *The Inner Reaches of Outer Space: Metaphor as Myth and as Religion*. Novato, CA: New World Library.

Real, Terrence. 1998. *I Don't Want to Talk About It*. Dublin, Ireland: Newleaf.

CHAPTER 10

Singer, Michael A. 1974. *The Search for Truth*. Alachua, FL: Shanti Publications, Inc.

Campbell, Joseph. 2012. *The Inner Reaches of Outer Space: Metaphor as Myth and as Religion.* Novato, CA: New World Library.

Fritz, Robert. 1989. *The Path of Least Resistance.* New York, NY: Fawcett.

Kapleau, Roshi P. 1989. *Three Pillars of Zen.* New York, NY: Alfred A. Knopf.

Moore, Robert, and Douglas Gillette. 1991. *King, Warrior, Magician, Lover: Rediscovering the Archetypes of the Mature Masculine.* London, England: HarperSanFrancisco.

Yogananda, Paramahansa. 2004. *Autobiography of a Yogi.* Los Angeles, CA: Self-Realization Fellowship.

Alphabetical

Anderson, Robert J., and William A. Adams. 2015. *Mastering Leadership: An Integrated Framework for Breakthrough Performance and Extraordinary Business Results.* Edited by Robert J. Anderson and William A. Adams. Nashville, TN: John Wiley & Sons.

Branden, Nathaniel. 1995. *Six Pillars of Self-Esteem.* New York, NY: Random House.

Brown, Brené. 2010. "The Power of Vulnerability." Ted.com. June 2010. https://www.ted.com/talks/brene_brown_the_power_of_vulnerability.

Campbell, J. 1994. *Hero's Journey.* Random House Value Publishing.

Campbell, Joseph. 2012. *The Inner Reaches of Outer Space: Metaphor as Myth and as Religion.* Novato, CA: New World Library.

Covey, Stephen R. 2013. *The 7 Habits of Highly Effective People.* 25th ed. London, England: Simon & Schuster.

Deutschman, Alan. 2007. *Change or Die: The Three Keys to Change at Work and in Life.* New York, NY: HarperCollins.

Duhigg, Charles. 2016. "What Google Learned from Its Quest to Build the Perfect Team." *The New York Times,* February 25, 2016. https://www.nytimes.com/2016/02/28/magazine/what-google-learned-from-its-quest-to-build-the-perfect-team.html.

Dweck, Carol S. 2008. *Mindset.* New York, NY: Ballantine Books.

Edwards Deming, W. 1988. *Out of the Crisis.* 2nd ed. Cambridge, England: Cambridge University Press.

Frankl, Viktor E. 2006. *Man's Search for Meaning.* 4th ed. Boston, MA: Beacon Press.

Fritz, Robert. 1989. *The Path of Least Resistance.* New York, NY: Fawcett.

Gladwell, Malcolm. 2009. *Outliers: The Story of Success.* Harlow, England: Penguin Books.

Goleman, Daniel. 2007. *Emotional Intelligence.* 10th ed. New York, NY: Bantam Books.

Hendricks, Gay. 1990. *Conscious Loving: The Journey to Co-Commitment.* New York, NY: Bantam Doubleday Dell Publishing Group.

————. 2010. *Five Wishes: How Answering One Simple Question Can Make Your Dreams Come True.* Novato, CA: New World Library.

"How Your Nervous System Works & Changes." 2021. Hubermanlab.com. January 4, 2021. https://hubermanlab.com/how-your-nervous-system-work s-and-changes/.

Jung, C. G. 1969. *Collected Works of C.g. Jung, Volume 9 (Part 1): Archetypes and the Collective Unconscious.* Edited by Gerhard Adler and R. F. C. Hull. Princeton, NJ: Princeton University Press.

Kahneman, Daniel. 2012. *Thinking, Fast and Slow.* Harlow, England: Penguin Books.

Kapleau, Roshi P. 1989. *Three Pillars of Zen.* New York, NY: Alfred A. Knopf.

Kegan, Robert. 1982. *Evolving Self: Problem and Process in Human Development.* London, England: Harvard University Press.

Kolb, David A. 1983. *Experiential Learning: Experience as the Source of Learning and Development.* Upper Saddle River, NJ: Financial Times Prentice Hall.

Livingston, J. Sterling. 2003. "Pygmalion in Management. 1969." *Harvard Business Review* 81 (1): 97–106.

Losada, Marcial, and Emily Heaphy. 2004. "The Role of Positivity and Connectivity in the Performance of Business Teams: A Nonlinear Dynamics Model." *The American Behavioral Scientist* 47 (6): 740–65.

Maslow, Abraham H. 2020. *A Theory of Human Motivation.* www.bnpublishing.com.

Mezirow, Jack. 1991. *Transformative Dimensions of Adult Learning.* London, England: Jossey-Bass.

Moore, Robert, and Douglas Gillette. 1991. *King, Warrior, Magician, Lover: Rediscovering the Archetypes of the Mature Masculine.* London, England: HarperSanFrancisco.

Ratner, Brett. 2000. *The Family Man*. USA: Universal Pictures.

Real, Terrence. 1998. *I Don't Want to Talk About It*. Dublin, Ireland: Newleaf.

Reichheld, Frederick, and Thomas Teal. 1996. *Loyalty Effect: The Hidden Force behind Growth, Profits and Lasting Value*. Boston, MA: Harvard Business Review Press.

Santos, Laurie. 2018. "The Science of Well-Being." March. https://www.coursera.org/learn/the-science-of-well-being.

Singer, Michael A. 1974. *The Search for Truth*. Alachua, FL: Shanti Publications, Inc.

Stone, Hal, and Sidra Winkelman. 1985. *Voice Dialogue*. Marina del Rey, CA: DeVorss.

Yogananda, Paramahansa. 2004. *Autobiography of a Yogi*. Los Angeles, CA: Self-Realization Fellowship.

ABOUT THE AUTHOR

DR. TONY DALOISIO was trained as an organizational psychologist and has practiced in that field for over thirty years, serving hundreds if not thousands of businesses, not-for-profit organizations, schools, hospitals, NGOs, and government agencies/ military operations. His work with them has incorporated strategic planning and implementation, change management, team development, executive coaching, and executive education. He has been a professor in the MBA program at Georgia Tech's Scheller College of Business, teaching leadership and organizational change. In the early parts of his career, which began in education, he was an inner-city high school principal where he advocated for disadvantaged youth. He received a PhD from the University of Connecticut in the field of Organization Psychology and Counseling Psychology, where he received a fellowship for his research in leadership style and taught graduate courses in psychology.

He was a lead instructor for the Center for Creative Leadership, where he facilitated the center's week-long flagship Leadership Development Program. In the mid-1980s, he was selected to a senior faculty position at the American Management Associations Presidents Group and innovative Master's in Management Program in New York City, New York. In the mid-nineties he spent four years at McKinsey and Co. in NYC traveling world-wide working with the top Fortune 50 companies' most senior executives designing and consulting in change management. He was instrumental in developing McKinsey's change practice.

In the early 2000s he forged a partnership with the late Dr. Stephen R. Covey, author of the blockbuster *New York Times* bestseller *The 7 Habits of Highly Effective People*, and then his son, Stephen M. R. Covey, to develop the consulting practice Principle Centered Leadership and teach *The 7 Habits* course around the world.

He founded and has been the CEO of Charter Oak Consulting group for thirty years. The company was listed as one of *Inc. Magazine*'s fastest-growing companies and has been awarded numerous citations for best-in-class consulting projects in various industries.

In 2017, he co-authored a highly acclaimed business book with Kendall Lyman entitled *Change the Way You Change*.

Tony lives in Washington Depot, Connecticut, and Atlanta, Georgia, with his wife, Teresa Hargrave. He is the proud father of Timo Daloisio and Morgan Daloisio and grandfather to Ryan, Julia, Addie, and James. He is enjoying his consulting practice with schools, NGOs, business startups, and a variety of mission-driven companies. He has a love of the outdoors, hiking, biking, and his favorite, golf.

With the publishing of this book, *The Journeyman Life*, he will be conducting training programs for men to lead groups of men interested in applying the ideas and tools from the book.

www.THEJOURNEYMANLIFE.com

www.CHANGETHEWAYYOUCHANGE.com

www.COCG.com

Made in the USA
Las Vegas, NV
29 January 2022